E.J. Attinelli

Numisgraphics

A List Of Catalogues, in which Occur Coins Or Medals, which Have Been Sold By

Auction in the United States

E.J. Attinelli

Numisgraphics
A List Of Catalogues, in which Occur Coins Or Medals, which Have Been Sold By Auction in the United States

ISBN/EAN: 9783743345607

Manufactured in Europe, USA, Canada, Australia, Japa

Cover: Foto ©Andreas Hilbeck / pixelio.de

Manufactured and distributed by brebook publishing software (www.brebook.com)

E.J. Attinelli

Numisgraphics

Books, Ancient Coins & Copperplate Engravings at Auction.

On THURSDAY and FRIDAY, June 12th and 13th,

Will be sold at GEORGE NICHOLS' Office, Court Street, Salem, Mass.

2000 vols Books, 300 valuable Coins, & 500 Copperplate Engravings,

belonging to the Estate of the late *BENJAMIN WATKINS, Esq.*—To be sold by order of Court.——Sale to commence on Thursday morning at 9 o'clock.

[illegible]

300 COINS—among which are the following.

Julius Caesar
Augustus Caesar
Tiberius Caesar
Claudius
Adrian, 2
[illegible]
An Athenian Coin
[illegible]
John
Edward 1st, 2
Henry 3d, 2 penny
do. 6th, 2
do. 8th, groat
Charles 2d, 4 crown
Edward the 6th, 3 crown
2 New-England Shillings, 1650
1 do. Three pence, 1652
3 do Two pence, 1662
[illegible] Roman Coins
3 [illegible] do
[All the above are Silver.]
3 Ducats, gold

500 COPPERPLATE ENGRAVINGS—among which are—viz.

1 Industry and Idleness by Hogarth
2 3 Pictures, Idle Apprentice, by do
3 3 do Industrious Apprentice do
4 [illegible] of Mt. Vesuvius
5 2 different views of Naples with a view of Mt Vesuvius
4 6 Pictures of Robinson Crusoe
5 Portrait of [illegible], Esq
6 do of [illegible] Mathews
7 do. of George 3d
8 do of George Whitefield
9 do. of Chief Justice Pratt
10 do of Benjamin [illegible]
11 [illegible] Scripture Prints
12 Battle of the Amazons
13 King George 1st and 2d & Queen Caroline
14 Birth place & Tomb of Shakespeare
15 Miranda
16 America
17 Harrich [illegible]
18 John Wilkes, Esq
19 Premium for the Concord
20 Massacre in Boston in 1770
21 Art of Love
22 L'etude de la Musique
23 Le premier [illegible]
24 Lettres
25 [illegible] of [illegible]
26 Cupid
27 Juno
28 Summer
29 La Vente de Nuits
30 La Leçon Maternelle

H. & W. H. DYER, Printers

A List of Catalogues,

IN WHICH OCCUR

COINS OR MEDALS,

WHICH HAVE BEEN SOLD BY AUCTION IN THE UNITED STATES,

ALSO,

A List of Catalogues or Price Lists of Coins,

ISSUED BY DEALERS,

ALSO,

A LIST OF VARIOUS PUBLICATIONS OF MORE OR LESS INTEREST TO
NUMISMATOLOGISTS, WHICH HAVE BEEN PUBLISHED IN
THE UNITED STATES,

COMPILED BY

E. J. ATTINELLI.

PRICE, TWO DOLLARS.

NEW YORK,
1876.

INDEX.

PREFACE.

This little work is with some diffidence presented to those interested in the Numismatology of the country ; as an aid to collectors of coin catalogues, or those desirous of forming a numismatic library relating to American coins or medals or subjects germane, which have been printed in this country.

The first part is devoted to a descriptive list of upwards of four hundred coin sale catalogues, arranged chronologically. An ample index to this part will be found at the end of the book.

In the second part will be found what are usually termed "Private Catalogues," which include catalogues by or for use of institutions or individuals, and dealers' price lists. These are also arranged chronologically.

The third part may be used as a hint in the formation of a numismatic library, devoted to American subjects ; this part is arranged alphabetically, generally by the author's name. No attempt has been made in the direction of foreign, mediæval, or ancient numismatology.

Information that will serve to fill up any of the many blank spaces, or of errors or omissions, will be thankfully received by the undersigned.

The writer acknowledges with gratitude the kind assistance received from many gentlemen, among whom it is proper to name the Messrs. McCoy, Jeremiah Colburn, Major C. P. Nichols, Chas. Chaplin, S. H. Chadbourne, J. N. T. Levick, and a prominent collector in this city who desires to remain unknown, but whose collection of American coin catalogues is the largest in the country.

To none, however, is more acknowledgment due than to WILLIAM POILLON, Jr., whose collection is unrivalled in the thoroughness with which it is priced and named, and in point of numbers, has but one superior. Ever courteous, ready to assist or give any information in his power ; to him are due my most sincere thanks.

E. J. ATTINELLI.

241 E. 57TH ST., NEW YORK.

Ten copies printed on large tinted paper.

ABBREVIATIONS, ETC.

p. - - - - Priced.
p. & n. - - - Priced and named.
P. P. - - - Prices printed.
P. N. - - - Prices and names printed.

In part I, the first space after the date, contains or is left to be filled in, with the name of the owner of the collection ; this rule has been in the cases of some of the most noted collections departed from, as in the McCoy, Mickley, etc. The next contains the name of the auctioneer, followed by the name of the place where sold. The next space is occupied by p. & n., where prices and names have been obtained by some collector. The next space gives number of days sale, followed by the number of pages, number of lots, and "gross proceeds" of the sale.

TO CATALOGUE COLLECTORS.

By marking in the margin opposite a catalogue, one of the characters in the following system, it has been found useful to easily, briefly, and clearly note the possession and condition of the catalogue :

○ Signifies its possession in good condition.
□ Signifies its possession in poor condition.
⦶ The perpendicular line added, denotes fully priced.
⊕ A horizontal line added, denotes priced and named.
⦶ Partial lines, thus, denote partly priced and partly named.

ERRATA.

Page 13.—The date on the right upper corner should have been 1858.
" 30.—Last line should read $360.00, instead of 380.00.
" 33.—Twenty-first line should read $360.00, instead of $30.00.

Auction Sale Catalogues.

In presenting this list of the Public Coin Sales which have taken place in the United States, the author believes that it will be acceptable to the reader to introduce the subject by having placed before him, through the gentlemanly courtesy of that indefatigable antiquarian and numismatist, Dr. Henry Wheatland, of Salem, Mass., a copy of what is possibly the *"First,"* announcement of a "Public Coin Sale" in this country, which that gentleman transcribed "verbatim et literatim" from the "Salem Gazette" of June 6th, 1828.

It is as follows:

"Administrator's Sale of Books, Furniture, Coins, &c. On Wednesday Next, will be sold at Public Auction at the

House of Benjamin Watkin, Esq. deceased, in
Marlborough Street,

All the Household Furniture of said deceased, consisting of Beds, Bedding, Carpets, Table Linen, China and Glassware, Parlour, Kitchen and Chamber Furniture, together with a great variety of other articles too numerous to particularize. Sale to commence at 9 o'clock A. M.

George Nichols, Auct.

And on Tuesday Next
At Geo. Nichols Office, Court St.

Will be sold all the books of said deceased comprising about 2500 vols.; 500 Copperplate Engravings, 350 Ancient Coins, Pamphlets, Newspapers, &c.

Also — 2d hand clothing, Silver Spoons, Porringers, &c., together with many other articles too numerous to particularize. Sale to commence at 9 o'clock, A. M., and to continue until the whole are sold. June 6."

1828.

O June 12 | Benj. H. Watkins | George Nichols | Salem |
| | 1 | 1 | 584 | $

To a gentleman of this city, well known to numismatists and bibliophiles, as well for the extent as for the select quality of his collections, both of coins and medals, as also of books, but whose modesty will not permit the use of his name, am I indebted for his courteous generosity in giving the use of his copy of the extremely rare, broadside sheet catalogue of the above described sale. Through this favor I have been enabled by the recently invented process of Photo-Litography, to present as a frontispiece, a *facsimile* of the catalogue on a reduced scale. A very few copies have also been made of the same size as the original, which is 18 inches in height.

As the announcement in the "Salem Gazette" inaugurates the first of a long line of public sales of coins in the United States, a few facts connected with the sale may not be inappropriate or uninteresting.

Mr. Benjamin H. Watkins, like many other citizens of Salem of his day, followed the sea in his earlier years, subsequently quitting that avocation, he married, and settling down, applied himself to the Dry Goods business in his native city, gratifying in his leisure hours his antiquarian predelictions by his search for and collection in a quiet modest way, such rarities of antiquity in the form of coins, books, engravings and other articles of curiosity or *vertú*, as came in his way. He was a man also noted for his extremely economical habits. His family having all preceeded him to "that bourne from whence no traveller returns," he became himself, in January, 1828, at the ripe old age of 75 years a prize to that insatiable *Old collector* of all, "Father Time."

Mr. Thomas Odell was the administrator of the estate; under his direction the collection of Mr. Watkins followed the apparently predestined fate of all private collections and passed under the hammer of the auctioneer.

Mr. John H. Nichols, then a youth of seventeen, made the catalogue, and, as a clerk assisted his father at the sale of the collection which, he informs me, that he is positive to the best of his recollection, did not bring a sum to exceed $1000. Mr. Nichols, who is now a resident of this city, purchased some of the coins for himself and became a numismatist, having a collection of his own at the present time.

To Dr. Wheatland and Mr. Nichols am I much indebted for their kind research and information through which I am enabled to lay before interested numismatologists this brief sketch of one of our earliest collectors in the United States.

1840.

Nov. 10 | | Aaron Levy | N. Y. |
        | | 1 | i | 215 | $

This is a sheet catalogue of autographs and medals. The last lot consists of "A collection of Napoleon Medals, commemorating the Military Events of his Reign."

1841.

÷ March 17 | | Bangs, Richards & Platt | N. Y. |
       | | 2 | 36 | 760 | $

A book catalogue. There is described as lot
"342 Medallion Busts of St. Peter and St. Paul."

¹ March 22 | | Royal Gurley | N. Y. |
       | | 4 | 40 | 1.140 | $

A book catalogue. The following is described as lot
"923 5 Cases, containing about 1200 castings of eminent men, medals, &c., &c."

1842.

May 17 | | F. J. Bearus | N. Y. |
       | | 46 | 2229 | $

This catalogue comprises books, stationery, etc. Lot 1724 is described as
"1 Masonic Medal."

1844

— April 20 | | Gurley & Hill | N. Y. |
       | | 1 | 1 | 330 | $

This is a sheet catalogue of books, etc. In the fourth column is a lot described as a "Box Italian Medallions."

1845.

Dec. 12 | Henry A. Brady | Gurley & Hill | N. Y. |
       | | 2 | 18 | 395 | $

Principally books. On pages 4 and 5, lots 59 to 64 are silver coins, lots 65 to 78 are copper coins.

1846.

○ April 22 | D. B. Warden | Horatio Hill | N. Y. |
       | | 2 | 20 | 691 | $

Principally books. On page 17, Lots 567 and 568 are described the "*Libertas Americana*" and "John Paul Jones" medals. A "Washington Medal," dated 1797, was sold as Lot 597* for 50 cts.

June 22 | | M. Thomas & Son | Phia. |
       | | 1 | 4 | 155 | $

A quarto catalogue.

Dec. 24 | | Bangs Richards & Platt | N. Y. |
       | | 1 | 1 | 453 | $

A broadside sheet catalogue of six columns. The lots not numbered, in the first column are the following, viz.

"22 Globe Medals."
"6 Medals. Reward of Merit."

1848.

March 22 | James Thompson | Dumont & Hosack | N. Y. |
       |p. | 1 | 55 | 1106 | $

A book catalogue. A lot subsequent to the numbered lots is described as "A Cabinet of Bronze Medals." Which, according to a ms. in a priced catalogue consisted of and sold at prices as follows:

Box No. 1	89 Medallions		$2.75
" 2	200 "		4.00
" 1*	Say 400 Bronze Medals, @ 14 cts. each		
" 2*	" 400 do do @ 15 cts. each		
" 3	" 300 do do @ 15 cts. each		
Cabinet $8.50.			

May 21 | Daniel E. Groux | Leonard & Cunningham | Boston |
| | 1 | 12 | 14 | $

In this catalogue, besides other curiosities and rarities, are described 30 cases of medals and 14 of coins, in which were contained 1026 of the former and 1333 of the latter.

1849.

March 8 | Robert Gilmor | Gibson & Co. | Baltimore |
| | 1 | 8 | 143 | $

The above is a catalogue of paintings, statuary, engravings, etc. Lot 143, however, is described as a "Lot of Greek and Roman Coins."

This gentleman had at one time one of the largest and finest collections of his day, which he disposed of at private sale. "From the Gilmor collection" was a recommendation, which immediately gave high character to a coin or medal.

May 15 | Gabriel Furman | Cooley & Keese | N. Y. |
| | 2 | 30 | 763 | $

In this catalogue there are 703 lots numbered and 60 not numbered.

This sale consisted principally of books.

Judge Furman, as he was familiarly termed, was born in Brooklyn, Long Island, New York, on the 23d of January 1800, and remained a batchelor until his death, which took place November 11th, 1854.

He was one that took an active part in the political questions of his day, and was elected a number of times to the State Legislature; in 1842 he ran as Lieut. Governor on the same ticket with Luther Bradish for Governor, but both were defeated.

Though acting so prominently in politics, his name will be better known to posterity as an energetic antiquarian, who devoted his researches particularly to Long Island and the city of his birth. His monuments exist in his "Notes on Brooklyn," as well as in other valuable and interesting contributions to Long Island History. The former work has since been republished, with memoirs of the author added by the "Faust Club" of Brooklyn, and which the reader will find quite interesting.

1851.

Feb. 20 | Lewis Roper | M. Thomas & Son | Phia. |
| p. & n. | 1 | 24 | 698 | $1172 47

The last 45 lots of this catalogue are autographs. This is, it is believed, the first coin sale in this country, in which sufficient interest was manifested by numismatists to take note of the prices paid for coins, and who were the purchasers.

April 22 | D. E. Groux | Leonard & Co. | Boston |
| p. | 1 | 8 | 148 | $34 66

There was an addenda sold by Ms. of 9 additional lots, but it had no coins.

June 11 | James Scrymgeour | M. B. Butler | N. Y. |
         | pp. | 2 | 15 | 454 | $13 25

This sale was principally furniture and books, among these are the following lots, viz.

        440   Medal of George III.
        444   1 do [Box] Old Coin,

The first lot sold for $6.25, the latter for $7.00.

1852.

March 23 | | Lyman & Rawdon | N. Y. |
         | p. | 1 | 1 | 205 | $

A broadside sheet, the lots are unnumbered, among them is a lot described as "A Cabinet of Monies."

April 28 | Philip Hone | E. H. Ludlow | N. Y. |
         | p. | 1 | 26 | 292 | $837 38

Mr. Hone was a well-known merchant, who became better known as Mayor of this city than as a numismatist.

The following is a summary of the sale:

       Paintings, ... $5910 00
       Coins and Medals, ...   837 88
       Numismatic Books, ...   166 50
       Statuary, ...   453 50
       Cabinet, ...   34 00

           Total $7401 88

Aug. 26 | | Leonard & Pierce | Boston |
         | | 1 | 1 | 212 | $

This is a large broadside sheet. The lots unnumbered. The last lot is described as "A collection of 123 Silver and Copper Coins."

Oct. 14 | John Dogget, Jr. | M. B. Butler | N. Y. |
         | | 1 | 8 | 179 | $

There are 74 lots that are numbered and 85 that are not. The collection was mainly paintings and autographs, on page 7 is a lot described as a "Specimen of Coins. French. 1."

Oct. 28 | | Lyman & Co. | N. Y. |
         | | 1 | 8 | 274 | $

This collection consists of books, etc. But 102 of the lots are numbered. The following two were the only lots of coins:

Lot "100, Jefferson Medal."
Lot "101, 10 Old American Dollars and two Half Dollars."

1854.

Nov. 22 | Jonathan M. Wainwright | Lyman & Co. | N. Y. |
| | | 38 | 1280 | $

Dec. 6 | Jonathan M. Wainwright | Lyman & Co. | N. Y. |
| | 2 | 16 | 531 | $

Though bearing different dates, the above are bound together. The second part is entitled a "Supplementary Catalogue" with pages numbered 1 to 16; the lots are not numbered; on Page 11 of the "Supplementary Catalogue" there are three lots, each of which is described as an "Old Roman Coin."

The writer has found that there were issues of each part separate of the preceding catalogue, as well as that of the two parts bound together. It is also possible that there may have been more pages and lots in the "Supplementary Catalogue" as the copy seen was at least lacking the cover at the end.

1855.

⊥ Jan. 10 | | Jordan & Norton | N. Y. |
| | 1 | 215 | $

A sheet catalogue of books, fancy goods, etc. In the first column is the following described:

"Lot of Medals, Crosses, etc."

· March 20 | Edward D. Ingraham | Thomas & Son | Phia. |
| | |184| 5158 | $

+ March 20 | Edward D. Ingraham | Thomas & Son | Phia. |
| | 47 | 1564 | $

+ March 20 | Edward D. Ingraham | Thomas & Son | Phia. |
| | 8 | 324 | $

The first catalogue comprises only books, the next or "Supplementary Catalogue" consists of books, autographs, and engravings, then an "Additional Supplementary Catalogue," following this great sale along, brings us to the following "Addendas" of

May 22 | Edward D. Ingraham | Thomas & Son | Phia. |
| | 1 | 12 | 168 | $

May 22 | Edward D. Ingraham | Thomas & Son | Phia. |
(Addenda) | p. | 1 | 1 | 37 | $28 50

This last addenda consists exclusively of coins.

| June 6 | Peter Flandin | Bangs Bros. & Co. | N. Y. |
| p. & n. | 1 | 14 | 230 | $733 52

This catalogue was, I believe, also issued with date of April 28.

June 12 | A. C. Kline | M. Thomas & Sons | Phia. |
                | p. | 2 | 92 | 1712 | $1753 29

June 12 | A. C. Kline | M. Thomas & Sons | Phia. |
    (Addenda.) | p. | 1 | 8 | 137 | $299 14

    ✓ Addenda bound in.

June 12 | A. C. Kline | M. Thomas & Sons | Phia. |
   (Supplement. Addenda)| p. | 1 | 1 | 5 | $10 37

    Some few books are included in the above collection. the "Supplementary Addenda" was sold from manuscript and has been since privately printed (25 copies.)

Nov. 5 | Henry A. Brady · | Bangs Bros. & Co. | N. Y. |
               | p. & n. | 6 |126| 2197 | $

○ Nov. 5 | Henry A. Brady | Bangs Bros. & Co. | N. Y. |
    (Addenda) | p. & n. | 1 | 4 | 93 | $45 60

    The above is a book sale catalogue with an "Addenda," in which the lots 2198 to 2240 are books, etc., followed by 50 lots of coins which are unnumbered.

1856.

Feb. 15 | | Bangs Bros. & Co. | N. Y. |
                | | 1 | 1 | 12 | $

    This is a sheet catalogue. in which were offered for sale, and quite extensively described, twelve cases containing 2504 coins and medallions. The method of offering coins in large lots and the manner of describing remind one forcibly of the style of the probable owner, Daniel E. Groux.

April 8 | | Leonard & Co. | Boston |
                | 1 | 1 | 273 | $

    This is a sheet catalogue of books, etc., the text terminating as follows: "Also several Silver and Copper Coins Medals. &c."

April 17 | Louis Borg | Bangs Bros. & Co. | N. Y. |
                | | 2 | | $

    This collection was withdrawn and not sold.

May 17 | | Leavitt Delisser & Co. | N. Y. |
               | p. | 1 | 1 | 52 | $98 05

    This was an "Addenda" to a book sale I believe. The lots are numbered 196 to 248.

May 17 | Addenda | Leavitt Delisser & Co. | N. Y. |
               | P. P. | 1 | 2 | 42 | $31 32

This was copied and printed from a manuscript which was imperfect; a few copies were privately printed, 5 on plain paper, and 25 on note paper, of which there have been destroyed 18 copies of the latter.

Sept. 16 | | Leonard & Co. | Boston |
                   | | 1 | 4 | 375 | $

This sale comprised 339 lots of books and 36 lots of coins.

Oct. 17 | Bangs Bros. & Co. | N. Y. |
             | p. & p. n. | 1 | 1 | 204 | $98 05

A large sheet catalogue of ancient Greek and Roman coins.

1858.

March 10 | | H. H. Leeds & Co. | N. Y. |
                 | | 1 | 14 | 216 | $

This was a sale of paintings etc. Lot 60, in this catalogue, is described as a " Valuable Collection of American Medals etc.," followed by a description in four lines of 41 medals. All the books and papers of H. H. Leeds & Co., which give details of their sales, having been sold for waste paper and destroyed, it will be impossible to obtain any information from that source with very few exceptions.

April 27 | | Herts & Moss | N. Y. |
            | p. | 1 | 16 | 240 | $2 62

This sale was principally paintings, book, and bric-a-brac. Lots 68, 69, and 70 were as follows:

"68 George Washington Independence Penny, 1783."
"69 George Washington President Penny, [North Wales.]"
"70 Beyer President of Hayti."

May 13 | Charles B. Norton | H. H. Leeds & Co. | N. Y. |
             | p. | 1 | 16 | 250 | $24 12

This sale comprised autographs, engravings, scrap books, coins, and medals, the latter of which were offered in lots 113 @ 120, 224 @ 232.

Oct. 26 | Frank H. Norton | Bangs Merwin & Co. | N. Y. |
            | p. & n. | 1 | 72 | 1144 | $164 17

The above catalogue has an "Addenda" bound in. It contains 48 lots of coins and medals, but the collection consists principally of books. The lots are not numbered consecutively, but in several divisions. In addition to the preceding "Addenda," there was the following small sheet, one separate.

Oct. 26 | Frank H. Norton | Bangs Merwin & Co. | N. Y. |
            | p. & n. | 1 | 1 | 31 | $19 75

Nov. 1 | Edward Cogan | Letter Biddings | Phia. |
                    | P. P. | 1 | 2 | 77 | $128.63

This sale, although perhaps not strictly an "auction sale," yet so closely approaches it, that it is given a place here. The coins were exhibited at Mr. Cogan's store, and bids for the various pieces were made in sealed letters, which letters, nineteen in number, were, in accordance with a previous understanding, opened on the 1st day of November; the highest bidder for any particular piece was to be regarded as the purchaser. The names of the bidders, with the corresponding numbers, are preserved.

Mr. Edward Cogan, whose name was brought conspicuously before the numismatic public by means of this sale, was born on the 5th of January, 1803, in the village of Walthamstow, Essex County, England.

He immigrated to this country with his family, in 1853, settling in Camden, a suburb of Philadelphia, and pursued the avocation of a picture dealer in the latter place. The following incident, which occurred in 1855, turned his attention to coins; a friend of his, named Ryan, casually exhibited to him an electrotype of the Washington Cent of 1791, while commenting on the value and rarity of the original, and of the scarcity of other pieces, he said to Mr. Cogan that he "would give him five dollars for a United States Cent of 1815." In his endeavors to procure one for his friend, Mr. Cogan commenced gathering all of the old cents which came in his way, keeping the various dates separate in *pill-boxes*. Casually showing these cents to acquaintances, he began making occasional sales and purchases, which transactions, increasing in frequency, induced him, in 1857, to devote his principal attention to numismatology, in Philadelphia. The sale of November 1st, having proved so great a success, stimulated many others to enter the business. It is from this fact that many have termed Mr. Cogan "The Father of the Coin Trade." In 1865, a wider field presenting itself in New York, he removed to this city and is now residing in Brooklyn. Mr. Cogan himself attributes the increased interest in numismatics to the change from copper to nickel cents.

Mr. Cogan's first printed catalogue is the one just mentioned and was but the precursor of many, as will be seen hereafter. Mr. Cogan's descriptions of the quality and rarity of coins have been made with a strict adherence to truth, and if he erred, it was generally in favor of the buyer rather than the seller. His scanty use of superlatives, will be remarked by all who look carefully over catalogues prepared by his pen.

1859.

Feb. 8 | Henry Pennington | M. Thomas & Sons | Phia. |
                    | | 3 | 34 | 971 | $

Feb. 10 | Henry Pennington | M. Thomas & Sons | Phia. |
                    | p. | 1 | 1 | 108 | $101.66

The sale of the 8th was a book sale to which that of the 10th was an addenda, this latter was a sheet. There were upward of 700 coins sold.

Feb. 28 | Henry Bogert | Bangs, Merwin & Co. | N. Y. |
                    | p. & n. | 6 | 93 | 1653 | $2198.47

Feb. 28 | Addenda | Bangs, Merwin & Co. | N. Y. |
| p. & n. | 1 | 11 | 331 | $309.50

> This collection was catalogued by Mr. Augustus B. Sage.
> Comprised in the above are 124 lots of books which brought $284.86.
> The addenda has the date Feb. 28th, but was sold March 5th.

March 7 | Charles B. Foote | Edward Cogan | Phia. |
| P. P. | 6 | 8 | 273 | $535.00

> This was not an auction sale, upset prices were placed on the pieces, competition was invited, with the result described. The ms. has been kindly loaned me by Mr. Foote, and an edition of 25 copies has been printed on tinted paper.

May 4, 5 | Wm. Leggett Bramhall | Bangs, Merwin & Co. | N.Y. |
| p. & n. | 2 | 31 | 595 | $352.65

| Addenda | Bangs, Merwin & Co. | N. Y. |
| p. & n. | 1 | 5 | 111 | $86.17

May 5 | Supplementary Addenda | Bangs, Merwin & Co. | N.Y. |
| P. P. | 1 | 1 | 26 | $6.12

> The latter addenda was sold from manuscript, which has since been privately printed, 5 copies on note and 20 on plain paper.

May 17 | | M. Thomas & Sons | Phia. |
| p. & n. | 1 | 1 | 528 | $252.79

> This is a broadside sheet. 197 lots were books. 266 numbered, and 65 unnumbered lots of coins and medals.

May 21 | Simon Gratz | Edward Cogan | Phia. |
| P. P. | 1 | 8 | 140 | $456.40

> This sale was conducted similarly to that of Mr. Foote's collection. An edition of 25 copies has been since printed from a ms. in the possession of Mr. Joseph N. T. Levick.

June 7 | James D. Foskett | Bangs, Merwin & Co. | N. Y. |
| p. & n. | 2 | 20 | 403 | $317.09

| Addenda | Bangs, Merwin & Co. | N. Y. |
| p. & n. | 1 | 1 | 21 | $14.89

> The addenda was sold from manuscript; a few copies have since been privately printed, 5 copies on note paper and 20 on plain paper.

June 21, 23 | John K. Curtis | Bangs, Merwin & Co. | N. Y. |
| p. & n. | 3 | 40 | 746 | $888.56

| Addenda | Bangs, Merwin & Co. | N. Y. |
| p. & n. | 1 | | 333 | $248.26

| Addenda No. 2 | Bangs, Merwin & Co. | N. Y. |
 , *)(o 5* ~~ | p. & n. | 1 | 2 | 40 | $37.63

The first addenda is bound in and forms part of the catalogue, while the second is a little separate sheet and printed on two sides.

The first 746 lots belonged to Mr. Curtis. The first addenda belonged to the following gentlemen, viz., Lots 1 @ 22, to A. M. Wilder; 22* to 50, to Thomas Walsh; 51 @ 59, to E. M. Camp, the remainder to Mr. Curtis.

June 24 | | Leonard & Co. | Boston |
 | p. | 1 | 10 | 119 | $16.16

The first 20 lots of this collection comprised all the coins. The remainder were paintings, etc.

July 27 | | Bangs, Merwin & Co. | N. Y. |
 | p. | 1 | 1 | 76 | $ 8.14

This is a small sheet. The collection comprising autographs and coins.

Oct. 28 | W. C. Tripler | W. C. Cook | Phia. |
 | p. & n. | 1 | 8 | 183 | $403.29

This was a collection formerly owned by Mr. W. C. Tripler. The collection was bought from him by Mr. Cogan, and sold by auction, at his store, from manuscript which has since been privately printed on tinted paper (25 copies), with prices and names.

Nov. 2 | Henry Whitmore | Bangs, Merwin & Co. | N. Y. |
 | p. & n. | 2 | 36 | 609 | $576.38

| Addenda | Bangs, Merwin & Co. | N. Y. |
 | p. & n. | 1 | 1 | 33 | $6.63

The addenda was sold from manuscript and has since been printed with the prices brought by each lot. There were 5 printed on note paper and 20 on plain paper.

Dec. 8 | | M. Thomas & Sons | Phia. |
 | | 1 | 1 | 47 | 418 | $

Principally books o which the lots are not numbered. There are 47 lots of coins.

Dec. 15 | *Eugene Wells Coll...* | Bangs, Merwin & Co. | N. Y. |
 | p. & n. | 1 | 14 | 459 | $78.57

Dec. 19 | Joseph N. T. Levick | Bangs, Merwin & Co.|N. Y.|
 | p. & n. | 2 | 32 | 976 | $1435.93

This catalogue was reprinted after the sale with the prices printed in, which each lot brought.

A few copies, the first published in this country, with the printed prices, were also issued on fine large paper.

Mr. Levick is a gentleman, well known among collectors and to the readers of the *Numismatic Journal*. To those who have not read his carefully prepared articles relative to some of the issues of this country, it need only be said that they have missed a treat. He is a pains-taking and thorough seeker after numismatic knowledge, devoting himself principally to American store cards, tokens, and political pieces. His knowledge relative to the first of these is probably unequalled; delighting to surprise his friends with a view of some new or rare pieces, after he has had them quietly put away for a time in his cabinet. Time or distance trouble him but little, if he but gets the idea that he will be rewarded, by turning up something new or unknown, and it is this ambition, which has led him sometimes into the not to be admired practice of "muling."

1860.

O Jan. 18| Alfred Hewitt *et al.* | Bangs, Merwin & Co. | N. Y. |
| p. & n. | 3 | 13 | 357 | $228.99

O | Addenda | Bangs, Merwin & Co. | N. Y. |
| p. & n. | | 7 | 205 | $

| Supplementary Addenda| Bangs, Merwin & Co. | N. Y. |
| P. P. | 1 | 1 | 3 | $5.30

The addenda is bound in, forming part of the catalogue.
The coins in the supplementary addenda were sold from manuscript, which has since been privately printed, 5 copies on note and 20 copies on plain paper.

⊕ Feb. 28 | Edward Groh | Bangs, Merwin & Co. | N. Y. |
| p. & n. | 2 | 34 | 825 | $418.70

| Addenda | Bangs, Merwin & Co. | N. Y. |
| p. & n. | 1 | 1 | 43 | $14.26

This addenda was issued at the time of the sale.
Mr. Edward Groh, the owner of this collection, was born in this city, June 3d, 1837, from boyhood up numismatics has occupied much of his attention; he is an active and diligent seeker after legitimate pieces of this country, and has probably the largest collection in the country, of what are generally termed "copperheads" or what might be more properly called "Rebellion tokens." He has also quite a cabinet of other coins and medals.
Mr. Groh was, as will be seen from the following copied from an original manuscript note, one of the originators of the New York Numismatic Society of which he is still an active member.

New York, March 8th, 1858.

DEAR SIR,

An informal meeting will be held at the house of Aug. B. Sage, 121 Essex St., for the purpose of taking the preliminary steps towards the organization of an Antiquarian Society in this city. You are earnestly requested to be present.

Respectfully,

Aug. B. Sage,
Henry O. Hart,
Jos. D. Foskett,
Edward Groh,
James Oliver.

Meeting, Monday }
Evening, March 15, }
7½ o'clock. }

To T. W. Lawrence.

⊘ March 26 | Wm. L. Bramhall | Geo. A. Leavitt & Co.|N.Y.|
| p. & n. | 2 | 24 | 862 | $455.35

A few lots in the above sale were coin publications and catalogues.

⊘ March 29 | Charles H. Morse | Draper, Morse & Co.|Boston|
| p. | 1 | 12 | 332 | $143.96

In addition to 266 lots of coins there are 66 lots of autographs. The amount
of proceeds I have taken from Mr. D. Parish Jr.'s list, as published in the
American Numismatic Journal, Vol. 1., of the benefit of which list I have
frequently availed myself. Mr. S. H. Chadbourne, himself a numismatist, was
bookkeeper for the above firm; he informs me that their books and papers he had
sold for "old junk." He thinks that the next described sale was for account of
Mr. George Pratt, but is not sure.

April 4 | Charles H. Morse | Draper, Morse & Co. | Boston |
| p. | 1 | 4 | 286 | $169.43

April 4|Geo. Pratt. Addenda | Draper, Morse & Co.|Boston|
| P. P. | 1 | | 11 | $49 95

In addition to 242 lots of coins, there are 44 lots of autographs. There were
also sold 11 lots of coins from manuscript, which has since been privately
printed, 5 copies on note paper and 20 copies on plain paper.

⊘ April 25 | Ezra Hill | Bangs, Merwin & Co. | N. Y. |
| p. & n. | 2 | 23 | 675 | $332.69

⊘ | Addenda | Bangs, Merwin & Co. | N. Y. |
| p. & n. | | 3 | 78 | $72.01

⊘ | Addenda | Bangs, Merwin & Co. | N. Y. |
| p. & n. | | 4 | 93 | $17.17

The first addenda forms part of the catalogue. The second was issued separately
at the time of the sale. The first addenda also belonged to Mr. Hill.

⊘ May 21 | Alfred Taylor | William C. Cook | Phia. |
| p. & n. | 2 | 48 | 1136 | $1934.88

The collection when sold was the property of Mr. Edward Cogan.

This catalogue was also printed on large paper. It was also reprinted with
prices, with change of number of pages and lots as follows.

May 21 | Edward Cogan | William C. Cook | Phia. |
| P. P. | 2 | 52 | 1137 | $1934.88

May 24 | Benj. J. Gallagher | Bangs, Merwin & Co. | N. Y. |
| p. & n. | 2 | 24 | 641 | $299 01

May 25 | Stevenson's Addenda | Bangs, Merwin & Co. | N.Y.|
| p. & n. | 1 | 49 | 149 | $36.33

Mr. Gallagher is a resident of this city, at present the Janitor of the New Court House. Mr. Gallagher had the good fortune to bring before the numismatic public one of the exceedingly rare Sommer Island pieces, which he bought with a lot of worthless pieces at a low figure.

May 30 | John K. Wiggins | Leonard & Co. | Boston |
| p. | 1 | 19 | 627 | $783.18

Mr. Wiggins was a well-known antiquarian bookseller and dealer in rare prints, as well as somewhat of a coin dealer. He was a resident of Boston.

June 15 | Edward Cogan | Wm. C. Cook | Phia. |
| p. & n. | | 16 | 662 | $

The sale was postponed to the 18th, but as the catalogue bears the date printed 15th, and has the 18th written over it, on which date the sale took place, it sometimes confuses those, who are not acquainted with the particulars. The collection is also known as the "Taylor and Watson Collection", they having been the former owners.

June 18 | Edward Cogan | Wm. C. Cook | Phia. |
| p. & n. | 1 | 16 | 662 | $524.87

See note above.

June 27 | W. E. Woodward & others| Leonard & Co.|Boston|
| p. | 2 | 11 | 721 | $70.64

Part of this collection was withdrawn from sale. As a whole, the sale was quite unsatisfactory to those interested.

W. Elliot Woodward, who was one of the principal owners of this collection, and who has since made himself so favorably and extensively known, not only to numismatists, but also to bibliophiles, was born on the 29th of November, 1825, at Oxford, Maine; he has, however, been for many years a resident of that portion of the city of Boston known as Roxbury, where he has kept an apothecary store. His ancestors were on both sides English, and among the earliest settlers of Massachusetts; on his maternal side, were the Cary's, who settled in Bridgewater, in 1634, while his paternal progenitors found a stopping place at Watertown, in 1635; therefore, Mr. Woodward may fairly entitle himself "a full-blooded Yankee." Near his present residence is "Muddy Brook," on which, with some evident pride, he points to an old tannery where his father and grandfather were employed at their trade.

Though cosmopolitan in character, Mr. Woodward has considerable of the Bostonian weakness of believing that city to be "The Hub," and the dome on the Capitol to be the centre, around which this world and the solar system revolves. His earlier educational advantages were only those of the common school. Of an inquiring and observing turn of mind, he instinctively turned to the minerals, birds, flowers, and insects of his native hills; gifted with an excellent memory, their names or localities once heard were seldom forgotten; even now his house contains many of these objects of his early search; old and curious coins, and odd things, or rarities, rapidly accummulated under his search, prosecuted with an indomitable energy, industry, and perseverance, which is untiring. "Go to the ant, thou sluggard," were never words addressed to him, for he is one of that restless busy kind, who scarcely ever think of rest. Having parted with a portion of his collection of coins, he at once set to seeking others of a choicer quality, again disposing of these, he developed into the "dealer"; having purchased the "Finotti" collection, he subsequently purchased the "Colburn", "Emery", "McCoy", and finally the "Mickley" cabinets. While thus engaged in the purchase and sale of these and others, too numerous to recapitulate, he was at the same time forming one of the finest private libraries of "Americana", publishing and reprinting fine or rare books; and as an instance of his success in that field, it may be stated that, having disposed of all the subscriptions to a work which he was about to issue, before it went to press, subscriptions like some of the fancy stocks on 'change commanded enormous premiums. He is a strong believer in printer's ink and does not use it parsimoniously, as an examination of the coin catalogues, prepared by him, will prove, and many of the notes from his familiarity with the subjects will be found interesting to numismatists.

Having disposed of his library, in 1867, as well as the "Mickley" collection, he turned his attention to real estate, in which, for several years, he has been one of, if not the heaviest operator in Boston, laying out many streets, and erecting buildings by the hundred.

While thus engaged he has found time, to present to numismatists his "18th Sale" and again formed a library equal to, if not superior to his previous one.

c June 28 | Jacob Glosser | Henry H. Leeds & Co. | N. Y. | | | | 16 | 513 | $

This catalogue is of the usual 8vo size, but is printed and bound differently, the width being of the usual height, and *vice versa*, the sale advertised did not take place; the collection was withdrawn, re-catalogued, and sold by Messrs. Bangs, Merwin & Co., on the 12th of July following. The following sheet "Supplementary Addenda" was issued at the same time as the preceding and shared its fortunes. The lots are numbered 514 to 571, both inclusive.

ɔ June 28 | Jacob Glosser | Henry H. Leeds & Co. | N. Y. | | | | 1 | 56 | $

July 11 | Charles H. Morse | Leonard & Co. | Boston | | | 2 | 27 | 1400 | $

E July 12 | Jacob Glosser | Bangs, Merwin & Co. | N. Y. | | p. & n. | 1 | 16 | 469 | $359.40

This catalogue has an addenda at the latter end of 80 lots, the first part is numbered to 388*, and was the collection offered at and withdrawn from H.H. Leeds & Co., on the 28th of June preceding, q. v.

July 31 | | Leonard & Co. | Boston |
                                        | p. | 1 | 8 | 590 | $200.57

Aug. 23 | | Bangs, Merwin & Co. | N. Y. |
                                        | | 1 | | | $

Books, autographs, and coins.

O Sept. 12 | Bramhall & Levick | Bangs, Merwin & Co. | N. Y. |
                                        | p. & n. | 3 | 40 | 1106 | $392.44

O Sept. 14 | H. G. Dwenger | Bangs, Merwin & Co. | N. Y. |
                                        | p. & n. | 1 | 4 | 150 | $57.89

The "Dwenger Collection" was sold as an "Addenda" to the Hill sale, as it has been heretofore termed, the actual owners not having been generally known.

Oct. 8 | Wm. E. Burton | Bangs, Merwin & Co. | N. Y. |
                                        | p. & n. | | 463 | 6151 | $

This great collection consisted principally of books. The coins (32 lots) are described on pp. 452 and 453.

The catalogue was also published on large paper. There were a number of addenda's (4 or 5), none of which, however, had any coins.

This collection formerly belonged to the well-known comedian, whose rare wit has served to while away many an otherwise tedious hour.

Oct. 17 | Charles H. Morse | Bangs, Merwin & Co. | N. Y. |
                                        | p. & n. | 2 | 20 | 807 | $460.34

This catalogue has printed on the inside of the covers and an attached leaf, a very interesting article on "Washington Coins," written by Dr. Augustine Shurtleff, which had been first published in the *Boston Transcript.* At first glance it might appear that the catalogue contains but 415 lots, which is but the second day's sale, the first day's sale consisting of 392 lots.

Oct. 18 | Edward Cogan | Wm. C. Cook | Phia. |
                                        | p. & n. | 2 | 31 | 891 | $1828.39

Some 10 or 12 copies of the above catalogue were printed on large paper. Subsequent to the sale, Mr. Joseph N. T. Levick had a supplement of 4 pages printed, giving the prices brought by each lot.

Oct. 23 | W. E. Woodward | Leonard & Co. | Boston |
                                        | p. & n. | 2 | 36 | 1222 | $240.53

Upward of 100 varieties of colonial pieces are separately described in this catalogue.

O Oct. 24 | Francis Joseph Klein | Bangs, Merwin & Co. | N.Y.
| p. & n. | 2 | 10 | 558 | $140.17

☉ | Addenda | Bangs, Merwin & Co. | N. Y. |
| p. & n. | | 6 | 180 | $60.33

Mr. Klein was born in the city of Coblenz on the Rhein, April 12th, 1812. He immigrated to this city in 1852, establishing himself in his avocation of watchmaker and jeweller. Subsequently, while on a visit to Europe, he became impressed, that ventures of coins purchased there might prove remunerative, if sold in this country. His private sales here were so; they were, however, of but small extent, but the sale just described and a subsequent one, disenchanted him, the results proving so unsatisfactory that he relinquished all ideas of any further attempts.

The "Addenda" is bound in and forms part of the catalogue, but did not belong to Mr. Klein, nor does he know, to whom it belonged.

O Nov. 21 | Prime & Haines | Bangs, Merwin & Co. | N.Y. |
| p. & n. | 2 | 26 | 866 | $ 725.48

This double collection consisted almost exclusively of American coins: succeeding lot 371 are a number of Pattern cents, the lots being distinguished by letters.

The owners were William C. Prime, the well-known writer, author, and antiquarian, and Benjamin Haines, a thriving merchant as well as an antiquarian. The former is a resident of this city, the latter of Elizabeth, N. J.

O Nov. 23 | John K. Curtis | Bangs, Merwin & Co. | N. Y. |
| p. & n. | 1 | 10 | 289 | $ 102.47

Mr. John K. Curtis, the owner of the above collection, was born in Deptford Road. Surrey Co., England, December 11th, 1828, and came with his parents in 1841 to this city; he soon after entered the employ of John Brock, a watchmaker and dealer in general curiosities, where he learnt his trade. In 1843 Mr. Curtis commenced a cabinet of his own, placing therein such choice pieces as his advantages favored him with. In 1857, having established himself on his own account, at No. 83 Bleecker St., his collection was brought into service as part stock for his new enterprise. Mr. Curtis was, as will be thus seen, one of the earliest in the field as a dealer in this country. The following year he purchased the "Siegfried collection" (from Easton, Pa.), for which he paid $700; at that time considered a large sum to pay for a single cabinet of coins. Mr. Curtis has published three dealers' catalogues, besides a number of others for auction sales, among which is that for the "Riley Museum," which collection was sold in January, 1864. Among some of the rare pieces, which have passed through his hands, is the unique "New Engl and" Massachusetts Cent described in "Dickeson," second edition. This piece he purchased from Mr. Dana, of Boston, and sold it to Mr. J. Colburn, who, with rare good judgment, presented it to the New England Numismatic Society, whose cabinet it now graces. Mr. Curtis was also the publisher of a number of well-known medals, one of them bearing the effigy of the well-known antiquarian, Mr. John Allan.

Dec. 13 | John K. Curtis | Bangs, Merwin & Co. | N.Y. |
                              | p. & n. | 2 | 18 | 446 | $473.28

○ Dec. 15 | John K. Curtis | Bangs, Merwin & Co. | N.Y. |
                              | p. & n. | 1 | 1 | 300 | $13.50

This is a large broadside sheet.

—Dec. 17 | Charles H. Morse | Bangs, Merwin & Co. | N. Y. |
                              | p. & n. | 2 | 15 | 896 | $

This catalogue of autographs, etc. should hardly be entitled a place among coin
catalogues, there being no coins in the sale.   An advertisement at the end, however, offers coins at private sale.

Dec. 26 | W. E. Woodward | Leonard & Co. | Boston |
                              | | 20 | 702 | $

The sale of this collection was postponed until January 8th, 1861.

1861.

Jan. 8 | W. E. Woodward | Leonard & Co. | Boston |
                              | p. & n. | 1 | 20 | 702 | $177.55

This catalogue is the same as the preceeding, but has the day and date printed
on a slip, which is pasted over the date of December 26. 1850.

○ Jan. 9 | Alfred S. Robinson | Leonard & Co. | Boston |
                              | p. & n. | 1 | 4 | 231 | $

This sale was principally autographs, there being but 29 lots of coins.

○ Jan. 28 | A. S. Robinson | Bangs, Merwin & Co. | N. Y. |
                              | p. & n. | 2 | 16 | 652 | $121.27

○ | Addenda | Bangs, Merwin & Co. | N. Y. |
                              | p. & n. | 1 | 2 | 53 | $12.97

Jan. 29 | Supplementary Addenda | Bangs, Merwin & Co. | N.Y. |
                              | P. P. | | 1 | 4 | $5.16

The first "Addenda" was issued previous to the sale; it is a small sheet, printed on
both sides.   The coins, described in the "Supplementary Addenda", were sold
from manuscript, which has since been privately printed: 5 copies on note paper
and 20 on plain paper.

O Féb. 5 | Wm. E. Lamb | Leonard & Co. | Boston |
                            | p. | 1 | 14 | 471 | $227.72

O Márch 7 | William King | Bangs, Merwin & Co. | N. Y. |
                            | p. & n. | 2 | 20 | 693 | $109.52

          O | Addenda | Bangs, Merwin & Co. | N. Y. |
                            | p. & n. | 1 | 1 | 36 | $25.86

The "Addenda" forms part of the catalogue. A note at the end of the catalogue
states "Also, about 100 lots of American and Foreign coin to be sold from manuscript" another note or "P. S." in lead pencil (in the catalogue which I have) says,
"none worth having." Has any one a copy of this ms.?

O March 21 | Francis J. Klein | Bangs, Merwin & Co. | N. Y. |
                            | p. & n. | 2 | 15 | 601 | $109 52

This was the portion of his collection, remaining after the sale of Oct. 24, 25, 1860.

O April 16 | A. S. Robinson | Leonard & Co. | Boston |
                            | p. & n. | 2 | 28 | 1134 | $403.00

April 17 | Addenda | Leonard & Co. | Boston |
                            | p. & n. | 1 | 3 | 166 | $25.67

April 29 | Joseph W. Wildey | Bangs, Merwin & Co. | N. Y. |
                            | p. & n. | 2 | 43 | 1085| $307.52

April 30 | A. S. Robinson | Bangs, Merwin & Co. | N. Y. |
                            | p. & n. | 1 | 1 | 33 | $

April 30 | Supplementary Addenda | Bangs, Merwin & Co. | N.Y.
                            | P.&N. | 1 | 1 | 20 | $9.05

The "Addenda" was printed on a small sheet and consists of autographs only;
it was issued prior to the sale. The "Supplementary Addenda" were sold from
manuscript, which has, with the prices, been since privately printed: 5 copies on
note and 20 on plain paper.

O May 29 | A. S. Robinson | Bangs, Merwin & Co. | N. Y. |
                            | p. & n. | 2 | 16 | 687 | $103.61

June 3 | C. Piazza | Bangs, Merwin & Co. | N. Y. |
                            | p. & n. | 2 | 16 | 650 | $78.60

July 29 | Daniel E. Groux | James Freemann | Phia. |
                            | | 1 | 51 | 219 | $

But a few lots were put up and bought in, and the sale was stopped.

1862.

Feb. 10 | Paul E. Fleury | Bangs, Merwin & Co. | N. Y. |
                            | p. & n. | 2 | 30 | 813 | $542.37

This collection comprised coins, autographs, books, etc.

March 19 | Satterlee and Mason | Bangs, Merwin & Co. | N.Y. |
                            | p. & n. | 2 | 31 | 714 | $320.27

This catalogue has an "Addenda," forming part of the bound catalogue. The collection belonged to Alfred H. Satterlee, G. B. Mason, Robt. Hewitt, and others.

March 25 | John K. Wiggin | Wm. C. Cook | Phia. |
                            | p. & n. | 2 | 36 | 975 | $1799.80

There is an "Addenda" at the end, forming part of the catalogue, which was sold first. This catalogue was re-issued after the sale, with the prices printed, and with a difference in the numbering of the pages as follows. Also a few copies on large paper.

March 25 | John K. Wiggin | Wm. C. Cook | Phia. |
                            | P. P. | 2 | 37 | 975 | $1799.80

       | do.   (Large Paper) | Wm. C. Cook | Phia. |
                            | P. P. | 2 | 37 | 975 | $1799.80

On the last page of the above is an "Addenda," the lots being distinguished by letters A to V. The numbered lots are 953.

March 26 | A. S. Robinson | Bangs, Merwin & Co. | N. Y. |
                            | p. & n. | 1 | 15 | 558 | $183.60

April 17 | George B. Davis | Bangs, Merwin & Co. | N. Y. |
                            | p. & n. | 2 | 24 | 649 | $309.49

A few copies of this catalogue were printed on tinted paper.

② April 22 | William A. Lilliendahl | Bangs, Merwin & Co. | N. Y.
| p. & n. | 2 | 27 | 466 | $11.96

③ | do.   Addenda | Bangs, Merwin & Co. | N. Y. |
| p. & n. | 1 | 3 | 74 | $22.33

The first above described was a book sale, but lots 406 to 466 are coins. The Addenda is coins exclusively.

④ May 8 | Satterlee & Mason | Bangs, Merwin & Co. | N. Y. |
| p. & n. | 2 | 26 | 643 | $250.41

This collection belonged to Messrs. A. H. Satterlee and George B. Mason.

⑤ May 14 | A. S. Robinson | Leonard & Co. | Boston |
| p. & n. | 1 | 16 | 588 | $502.92

⑥ May 26 | William A. Lilliendahl | Bangs, Merwin & Co. | N. Y
| p. & n. | 3 | 53 | 1230 | $2241.00

✓ This catalogue was issued subsequent to the sale, with printed prices.

This collection, one of the finest presented for public sale up to that time, was, as already stated, the property of Mr. William A. Lilliendahl, who was actively engaged in mercantile business. A gentleman of affable and genial disposition, abounding in good humor, of very sanguine temperament, with fine cultivated tastes, which directed him promptly in the selection of fine or rare pieces for his cabinet, as the quality of the coins, in this as well as those sold in his collection in 1863, gives amplest evidence.

Mr. Strobridge, who prepared this catalogue, and whose name as a most enthusiastic admirer of *antiques*, whether in the form of coins, bronzes, engraved gems or ceramic ware, has since become through the catalogues prepared by him, inseparably connected with some of the finest collections sold in this country.

The following brief sketch of this gentleman may perhaps not be here inappropriate.

William Harvey Strobridge first saw the light on the 9th day of January, 1822, in the town of Barnet, Caledonia County, amid the Green Mountains of Vermont. Having passed there the earlier period of youth, he subsequently, with the noted versatility of the Eastern people, became employed in various occupations. Endowed with tastes, which led him to the study and acquisition of the antique coins of Greece and Rome, he next became interested with those of Great Britain, then those of his own country and of Continental Europe. His large and fine cabinet of ancient coins, etc., he sold to Mr. W. A. Lilliendahl.

Mr. Strobridge's familiarity with numismatics, his extensive fund of tale and anecdote, the convenient locality of his office, soon rendered the latter a centre to which those of congenial tastes were rapidly attracted; there to discuss about, barter, or otherwise dispose of their coins or *bric-a-brac*.

Thus did he gradually, undesignedly, but naturally drift into the profession and pursuits of an antiquary, to which he now exclusively devotes himself. His extensive reading and retentive memory eminently fit him, to cope with the many forms, shapes, and varieties in which the products of antiquity present themselves.

Fine examples of his work and ability are shown in the catalogues of the "Lilliendahl collection" sold in 1863, the Middleton, Gay, Stenz, the several Holley collections, and others, which will well repay the studious numismatist to examine.

June 17 | | H. H. Leeds & Co. | N. Y |
| p. | 1 | 11 | 96 | $

Lots 90 to 96 are coins and medals.

○ July 30 | Henry Cook | D. F. McGilvray & Co. | Boston |
| p. & n. | 1 | 31 | 695 | $430.79

Mr. Cook is a resident of Boston, a shoemaker by trade, which occupation he pursues—supplementing that with that of a dealer in coins; he is also the author of a little pamphlet relating to coins.

Aug. 7 | Satterlee & Mason | Bangs, Merwin & Co. | N. Y. |
| p. & n. | 1 | 19 | 490 | $198.40

○ Sept. 22 | | Bangs, Merwin & Co. | N. Y. |
| p. & n. | 1 | 15 | 484 | $159.59

① Nov. 11 | Rev. J. M. Finotti | Bangs, Merwin & Co. | N. Y. |
| p. & n. | 4 | 88 | 1908 | $3751.43

Copies of the above catalogue, cut and uncut, were issued after the sale, with printed prices.

10 copies with printed prices were also issued on large paper.

This collection, though really belonging to Mr. W. Elliot Woodward of Roxbury, Massachusetts, was, when sold, presented to the numismatic world as the "Finotti Collection." Mr. Woodward, was well-known for his readiness to purchase and sell any collection, no matter how great.

The undoubted success he met with, in presenting to the public some of the largest and finest in the United States, are all matters too well known, to require any further elucidation. This was his first sale in New York.

○ Nov. 28 | William Young | Bangs, Merwin & Co. | N. Y. |
| p. & n. | 1 | 16 | 427 | $203.49

⌐ Dec. 16 | A. H. Satterlee | Bangs, Merwin & Co. | N. Y. |
| p. & n. | 1 | 30 | 416 | $406.20

This collection was composed of presidential or political pieces.

Mr. Satterlee was the well-known author of that desirable work, entitled: "The Presidential Series," of which this collection formed the base in its preparation.

His social disposition, it is deeply to be regretted, led him to an early grave. His abilities gave promise of valuable contributions to seekers after numismatic knowledge.

1863.

⊙ Ján. 19 | Rev. M. Hill | James C. McGuire | Washington |
                    | | | 13 | 340 | $

The sale of the above collection was postponed until the 26th.

⦾ Ján. 19 | Benjamin Haines | Bangs, Merwin & Co. | N. Y. |
                    | p. & n. | 5 | 110 | 2382 | $5375.30

✓ This catalogue was also issued subsequent to the sale, with printed prices.
Also printed on large paper.

Ján. 26 | Rev. M. Hill | James C. McGuire | Washington |
                              | p. | 1 | 3 | 340 | $297.79

This catalogue is the same as that of the 19th, only differing in the date; the
"26th" being sometimes on a little slip of paper, which is pasted over the "19th."

⊙ Ján. 29 | Wm. H. Bridgens | Bangs, Merwin & Co. | N. Y. |
                              | p. & n. | 2 | 32 | 899 | $309.00

              | Addenda | Bangs, Merwin & Co. | N. Y. |
                              | p. & n. | | 92 | $56.77

This collection belonged to the well-known die-sinker, whose medals are
numerous and fine.

⦾ Feb. 4 | Blake | Bangs, Merwin & Co. | N. Y. |
                              | p. & n. | 1 | 24 | 413 | $206.22

     ⊙ | Addenda | Bangs, Merwin & Co. | N. Y. |
                              | p. & n. | 1 | 3 | 92 | $71.85

This collection is the one known as the "Turkish Collection."
The lots in the "addenda" are numbered from 414 to 505.

⊙ March 9 | Alfred S. Hunter | Wm. L. Wall & Co. | Washington.
                    | | 1 | 96 | 2905 | $

This was principally a book sale, purporting to be "Washington's Library." It
has coins on page 91, commencing with lot 2733.

March 9 | | Bangs, Merwin & Co. | N. Y. |
      | p. | 2 | 28 | 745 | $

On pages 12 and 13 are described several bronze medals.

March 18 | | S. G. Hubbard | Cinn. |
      | | 1 | 1 | 682 | $

This is a large broadside sheet, comprising books and coins.

March 24 | Henry A. Smith | Bangs, Merwin & Co. | N. Y. |
      | p. & n. | 3 | 80 | 1627 | $1959.62

      | Addenda bound in | | |
      | p. & n. | 1 | 2 | 47 | $64.50

March 26 | Addenda | Bangs, Merwin & Co. | N. Y. |
      | | 1 | 1 | 100 | $

This catalogue contains, besides some rare pieces, a large collection of store cards. Mr. W. E. Woodward contributed considerably towards the above collection. The first addenda is bound in, forming part of the catalogue. The sale of the second addenda was postponed until April 8th.

March 27 | W. E. Woodward | F. J. Sheldon | Providence |
      | p. & n. | 1 | 13 | 332 | $304.08

Also published on large paper.

April 7 | Edward Cogan | Bangs, Merwin & Co. | N. Y. |
      | p. & n. | 2 | 37 | 1182 | $2593.36

Through an error of the printer, the date "7th and 8th May" was printed on the covers, which was corrected by pasting a little slip with the date of "7th and 8th April" over the other. Mr. Cogan's card on the inside, with date of March 12th, plainly showing the error.

This catalogue was also issued with a change of covers, which bear the word **"Priced"** in addition, but which are not priced unless done with the pen.

April 8 | Addenda | Bangs, Merwin & Co. | N. Y. |
      | p. & n. | 1 | 1 | 100 | $

This "Addenda" is the same as that of the 26th of March, with the exception of the change of date.

April 10 | | Thomas & Sons | Phia. |
                              | | 1 | 1 | 200 | $

This is a large broadside sheet, containing 140 lots of coins, the remainder are engravings and books. There is a copy which is printed alike on both sides.

ⱭApril 28 | W. E. Woodward | Bangs, Merwin & Co. | N. Y.
                              | p. & n. | 4 | 112 | 2569 | $4024.66

This was Mr. Woodward's second semi-annual sale, comprising selections from the collections of the following gentlemen, whose collections he had purchased, viz.:

> Henry M. Brooks, Esq.,
> Jeremiah Colburn, Esq.,
> Rev. J. M. Finotti,
> Dr. Edward M. Field,
> Dr. Augustine Shurtleff.

This sale consisted exclusively of American pieces, including Colonials and a large selection of store cards.

After the sale the catalogue was reprinted with prices; the sheets cut and uncut. Also a few copies on large paper. The following sheet was an addenda to the preceding sale.

O May 1 | A. S. Robinson | Bangs, Merwin & Co. | N. Y. |
                              | p. & n. | 1 | 1 | 100 | $27.25

O May 7 | Edward Cogan | Bangs, Merwin & Co. | N. Y. |
                              | | | 37 | 1182 | $

See April 7, 8, last.

⁷ June 9 | Henry A. Muhlenberg | Bangs, Merwin & Co.|N. Y.
                              | p. & n. | 2 | 78 | 1549 | $2514.54

      ⅃ | Addenda | Bangs, Merwin & Co. | N. Y.
                              | p. & n. | 1 | 4 | 110 | $58.67

This collection consisted quite largely of ancient coins. The addenda is bound in the catalogue.

O June 9 | | A. J. Harrison | Bangs, Merwin & Co. | N. Y. |
                              | p. & n. | 1 | 12 | 356 | $251.80

This is a separate catalogue, having the word "Addenda" printed at the top and although it bears the date of the 9th, it was not sold until the 11th, being "a continuation of the sale of the late Hon. Henry A. Muhlenberg's Collection."

The following was another "Addenda" printed on a small broad sheet.

◡ June 11 | Charles W. Betts | Bangs, Merwin & Co. | N. Y. |
　　　　　　　　　　　　　| p. & n. | 1 | 1 | 28 | $20.46

This gentleman is now a prosperous lawyer in this city. While at college he was somewhat interested in numismatics, and occupied some of his leisure hours as an amateur die-sinker.

◡ June 18 | John M. Jewell | Bangs, Merwin & Co. | N. Y. |
　　　　　　　　　　　　　| p. & n. | 1 | 19 | 438 | $105.25

The following was a sheet "Addenda."

0 June 18 | A. S. Robinson | Bangs, Merwin & Co. | N. Y. |
　　　　　　　　　　　　　| p. & n. | 1 | 1 | 100 | $31.37

0 June 23 | 　　　　　　　| Bangs, Merwin & Co. | N. Y. |
　　　　　　　　　　　　　| p. & n. | 1 | 10 | 192 | $5.36

This sale consisted principally of antiques, etc. Lots 121 to 126, inclusive, were medals.

The total proceeds of the sale were $439.19.

⦽ June 24 | Rev. James Eddy | Leonard & Co. | Boston. |
　　　　　　　　　　　　　| p. & n. | 1 | 3 | 203 | $115.85

The first 143 lots are coins and medals, the remainder photographs and photograph albums.

Sept. 8 | Lorenzo H. Abbey | Henry H. Leeds & Co. | N. Y.
　　　　　　　　　　　　　| p. & n. | 1 | 1 | 46 | $59.48

This was a coin sale, succeeding one of furniture, etc. The owner of the coins was the gentleman whose name is perpetuated in the celebrated "Abbey Cent" of 1799, which, notwithstanding so many years have elapsed, since it was brought to the notice of the numismatic public, still maintains its position as "one of the finest known."

Mr. Abbey is a native of this State, having been born in Herkimer Co., on the 14th of January, 1823. He has long been a resident of this city, carrying on an extensive business in needles, fishing-hooks, and tackle. His introduction to numismatology occurred through the following incident :

Mr. John Martense, a friend of his and a numismatist, having a duplicate uncirculated cent of 1826, presented it to Mr. Abbey, stating that it was worth about $5.00; being somewhat incredulous, he took it to Mr. Sage, who at once offered Mr. Abbey $7.00 for the cent; somewhat astonished by finding fine coins to have such a value, he at once applied himself in diligent search for others, and with some considerable success. The very next day he procured from a grocer's till the rare "large head Nova Eboraca."

The "99" cent above alluded to, he bought for $25.00 from Mr. Rogers in Fulton St., who had bought it from a countryman for $2.00. Among other pieces he thus brought to the knowledge of numismatists, were the "Washington Half Dollars" in copper, the 1802 Half Dime, subsequently sold in Mr. Lilliendahl's sale for $380.00, and other fine or rare pieces.

⍭ Sept. 15 | J. P. Leavitt | Bangs, Merwin & Co. | N. Y.
                            | p. & n. | 3 | 19 | 1862 | $1622.07

⍉ Sept. 22 | George F. Seavey | Bangs, Merwin & Co. | N.Y. |
                            | p. & n. | 2 | 40 | 1000 | $3407.79

This was a collection of exclusively American coins. The catalogue was reprinted, subsequent to the sale, with prices; a few copies were also issued,
printed on large paper. The reprint is 45 pages.

○ Oct. 7 | Nathan Brown & Jackson|Bangs, Mervin & Co.|N.Y.
                            | p. & n. | 1 | 26 | 461 | $479.25

          | Addenda | Bangs, Merwin & Co. | N. Y. |
                            | P. P. | 1 | 1 | 29 | $8.43

Lots 297 @ 344 were the property of Rev. Nathan Brown of Japan.
The above addenda was sold from manuscript, it has been since privately
printed; 5 copies on note paper and 20 on plain paper.

Oct. 9 | | Thomas & Son | Phia. |
                            | p. | 1 | 1 | 301 | $

This is a large sheet; the lots are not numbered; in the last column are two
coins.

⍭ Oct. 20 | W. E. Woodward's 3d|Bangs, Merwin & Co.|N. Y.|
                      · | p. & n. | 5 | 160 | 3202 | $4752.77

♂ Oct. 24. | Addenda | Bangs, Merwin & Co. | N. Y. |
                            | p. & n. | | 4 | 117 | $

The above catalogue and "addenda" were issued, bound together as well as
separately. The "addenda" is numbered 3203 to 3319.
After the sale the whole together was reprinted with prices, cut and uncut
copies (50 of the latter).
10 copies were also issued, printed on large paper, @ $10.00 per copy.

⍉ Oct. 20 | Jeremiah Colburn | Bangs, Merwin & Co. | N. Y. |
                            | P. P. | | 56 | 762 | $

This catalogue comprises that portion of the preceding collection, formerly
owned by Mr. Jeremiah Colburn of Boston.
Mr. Jeremiah Colburn, the former owner of this fine collection, is a native of
Massachusetts, where he was born on the 12th of January, 1815, the only year
since the establishment of the U. S. Mint in which no "cents" were coined. Mr.
Colburn began the collection of coins at the age of fifteen and is still not only a
collector, but a numismatic student. Many of the articles on American coins
and coinage under the head of "Notes and Queries" in the N. Y. Historical

Magazine, during the year 1857 and since, were the contributions of Mr. Colburn. In 1860 he was one of the founders of the Boston Numismatic Society, of which body he became Vice-President and subsequently the President. In 1871, he assumed with some other numismatic friends, the publication of the American Journal of Numismatics, which was thus transferred from New York to Boston. Besides the honors, which have so deservedly been conferred by numismatists, Mr. Colburn was also in 1869 made the recipient of the degree of *A. M.* from Williams College. May many years be yet spared to him, in which to throw light upon the uncertain origins of some of the early coins and tokens of our native country.

50 copies of this catalogue (uncut) were printed with the prices, and issued after the sales as also 12 copies on large paper, published at $5.00.

Nov. 3 | Mary Ann Bacon | Thomas & Sons | Phia. |
                 | p. & n. | 1 | 1 | 36 | $149.19

Nov. 7 | Henry H. Leeds & Co. | N. Y. |
                 | p. & n. | 1 | 1 | 38 | $68.17

Copies of this sheet catalogue were printed on both, white and blue paper. There was an additional lot sold as "38" Set of Cents 1795 to 1856."

Nov. 10 | Thomas & Sons | Phia. |
                 | p. & n. | 3 | 34 | 695 | $48.00

This was a book-sale, but on page 7 is a lot of 48 medals, which were sold for $48.00.

Nov. 21 | E. J. Attinelli | H. H. Leeds & Co. | N. Y. |
        | | | 4 | 148 | $

The sale of this collection was postponed until the 25th, when the same catalogue was used, the date only changed by pen or pencil.

⊙ Nov. 24 | Henry Cook | Leonard & Co. | Boston. |
                 | p. & n. | 1 | 4 | 422 | $149.23

This catalogue is a large quarto.
D Addenda of 36 sales,

Nov. 25 | E. J. Attinelli | H. H. Leeds & Co. | N. Y. |
                 | p. & n. | 1 | 4 | 148 | $59.58

Nov. 25 | Addenda | H. H. Leeds & Co. | N. Y. |
                 | P. & N. | 1 | 1 | 4 | $5.37

This addenda was sold from manuscript at the sale, but has since been privately printed with prices and names; 5 copies on note and 20 on plain paper.

Nov. 25 | Charles A. Junghams | S. G. Hubbard | Cinn. |
                        | | 1 | 1 | 216 | $

This is a large broadside sheet.

Dec. 1 | George H. Blake | Letter Biddings. | Salem |
                        | | | 2 | 88 | $

See Jan. 2, 1864.

Dec. 5 | | H. H. Leeds & Co. | N. Y. |
                        | p. | 1 | 8 | 177 | $

This catalogue has no coins, but a notice on the title page gives the information
that "A choice collection of Ancient Silver Coins, Medals, &c., will be sold
immediately after the furniture." The following was sold from manuscript,
from which 25 copies have since been privately printed.

Dec. 5 | | H. H. Leeds & Co. | N. Y. |
                        | P. | 1 | 8 | 145 | $462.22

⊕ Dec. 15 | William A. Lilliendahl | Bangs, Merwin & Co. | N.Y.
                        | p. & n. | 3 | 80 | 1388 | $3799.98

        ⊖ | Addenda | Bangs, Merwin & Co. | N. Y. |
                        | p. & n. | 1 | 2 | 75 | $91 87

The addenda is bound in the catalogue, which was issued both, cut and uncut.
It was in this collection that was sold the "Half Dime of 1802," which brought the
sum of $30; a sum unequalled to this day for that coin.
        $360—

Dec. 23 | W. E. Woodward | F. J. Sheldon | Providence. |
                        | p. & n. | 1 | 16 | 504 | $

Mr. Woodward's second sale in that city, and the success it met, reflects credit
on the numismatists there, as well as the auctioneer.

◊ Dec. 24 | | H. H. Leeds & Co. | N. Y. |
                        | p. & n. | 1 | 8 | 68 | $

This sale consisted principally of paintings and jewelry.
The following lots were the only ones of interest to numismatists, as taken from
the catalogue, with prices for which sold, and names of purchasers, added.

Hanna,	$1.75.	Lot 27.	Box of medals. Series of sovereigns of France, England, etc.
Attinelli, *ea.*,	$0.15.	" 28.	A box containing coins dug up in Morocco, Tunis, etc.
Cash, *ea.*,	$0.11½.	" 29.	Bag, ancient coins (some very rare), with descriptions, etc.
Monroe, *ea.*,	$0.15.	" 30.	Bag, miscellaneous coins, money pieces, etc.
Cash,	$1.00.	" 41.	Mexican coin, pure silver 1813.
Cash,	$2.00.	" 49.	Medal of Pope Gregory XVI., obverse St. Peters.

Dec. 24 | E. J. Attinelli | H. H. Leeds & Co. | N. Y. |
| p. & n. | 1 | 1 | 117 | $44.17

This is a long narrow sheet, the lots commencing at 101. The preceding catalogue terminates with lot "68."

Dec. 28 | J. A. Wright, F. S. Edwards | Bangs, Merwin & Co. | N.Y
| p. & n. | 2 | 29 | 702 | $1641.59

This collection was formed from the cabinets of Ex-Gov. Wright of Indiana, Dr. Edwards, Mr. L. Linchland, and others. The catalogue was made by Mr. Strobridge, and was issued cut and uncut, a few copies interleaved, also a few copies on large paper.

1864.

Jan. 2 | George H. Blake | Letter Biddings. | Salem |
| p. & n. | 1 | 2 | 88 | $62.17

This sale, like that of Mr. Cogan's of Nov. 1st, 1858, was conducted by sealed bids; the catalogue was issued Dec. 8th, 1863, inviting bids.

Jan. 5 | | Leonard & Co. | Boston |
| p. & n. | 1 | 6 | 331 | $233.00

Principally French medals.

Jan. 6 | John King | Leonard & Co. | Boston |
| | | 3 | 201 | $

This collection was withdrawn and not sold.

Jan. 12 | J. P. W. Neff, · | Bangs, Merwin & Co. | N. Y. |
| p. & n. | 3 | 79 | 1715 | $2359.50

Jan. 13 | Thomas Riley | A. J. Bleecker & Co. | N. Y. |
| p. & n. | 4 | 32 | 1097 | $1169.55

Jan. 13 | Addenda | A. J. Bleecker & Co. | N. Y. |
                             | P. P. | 1 | 1 | 102 | $59.25

This sale consisted principally of coins; there were a few curiosities in both the catalogue and addenda. The latter was sold from manuscript which, a few days after the sale, was printed with the prices for which the lots were sold. There were 75 copies printed. There was quite an interesting circular, announcing the forthcoming sale, issued a few days previous, on a sheet about 8½ x 10½ inches.

Ø Jan. 13 | | George A. Leavitt | N. Y. |
                             | | | 16 | 450 |

The sale of this collection was postponed to the 20th, in consequence of three coin sales in this city, being fixed for one time, it was sensibly deemed wiser to postpone one of them.

① Jan. 20 | | Geo. A. Leavitt | N. Y. |
                             | p. & n. | 1 | 16 | 450 | $164.56

Feb. 24 | Walter Deakins | Wm. A. Butters & Co. | Chicago |
                             | p. & n. | 1 | 18 | 433 | $27.35

This sale consisted principally of books. There were 113 lots of coins, which brought the above named sum, as taken from a priced catalogue. The books and papers of the auctioneers were all destroyed in the great fire of October 9th, 1871.

O March 15 | Great Western Sanitary Fair | S. G. Hubbard | Cinn.
                             | p. & n. | 1 | 39 | 825 | $242.75

This sale consisted principally of autographs, among which was the original "Amnesty Proclamation of President Lincoln," which brought $150. The lots of coins commence on page 30, Lot 577, extending to Lot 727 on page 33. The principal portion of the collection were mint medals, donated by the late Hon. S. P. Chase. The gross proceeds from the sale of the coins was, as given above, $242.75.
There was a small sheet addenda of 23 lots, but it included no coins.

◌ March 17 | | Thomas & Sons | Phia. |
                             | p. | 1 | 1 | 199 | $73.24

This sale comprised principally books, of which there were 138 unnumbered lots, and 61 lots of coins, which were numbered. The whole printed on a single broadside sheet.

C March 30 | W. E. Woodward | F. J. Sheldon | Providence |
                             | p. & n. | 1 | 23 | 574 | $589.96

Mr. Woodward's second sale in Providence.

March 30 | | Thomas & Sons | Phia. |
                                    | | 1 | 13 | 196 | $

This is a catalogue of books, having one lot on the last page, described as follows:
"Lot of 14 Coins and Continental Money."

April 19 | Henry Cook, *et al* | D. F. McGilvray & Co.|Boston|
                        | p. & n. | 1 | 4 | 392 | $104.51

        | Addenda | D. F. McGilvray & Co. | Boston |
                        | p. & n. | 1 | 1 | 8 | $5.20

This is a quarto size catalogue, illustrated. A number of the lots were not sold.
The addenda was sold from manuscript, which has since been privately
printed; 5 copies on note, and 20 on plain paper.

May 2 | John Allan | Bangs, Merwin & Co. | N. Y. |
                        | p. & n. | 12 | 344 | 5278 | $

This catalogue, which consisted largely of books and curiosities of various
kinds, was issued in various portions, separately, as well as that described above;
some copies with an addenda bound in; an addenda of "Missals" separate,
another sheet, addenda, of "Autographs." A supplement was published subsequent to the sale by Mr. Wm. Gowans, giving prices and names of purchasers.
That portion of the catalogue, which comprised the coins, viz., lots 4140 to 4558,
pages 297 to 312, was also issued separately, or detached from the remaining
portions. The date, May 2d, is on a slip, pasted over the date of April 25.
Mr. Allan was so noted an antiquarian as to require no further mention from me.

May 12 | | Leonard & Co. | Boston |
                        | p. & n. | 1 | 8 | 247 | $210.83

May 17 | John F. McCoy | G. A. Leavitt | N. Y. |
                        | p. & n. | 5 | 160 | 3122 | $13,010.60

        | W. E. Woodward's Addenda | G. A. Leavitt |N. Y.|
                        | p. & n. | 1 | 1 | 9 | $

May 21 | C. W. Betts, Addenda | G. A. Leavitt | N. Y. |
                        | p. & n. | 1 | 4 | 45 | .$33.30

This catalogue was also issued with a different cover, having the words
"Priced Catalogue," etc. This noted collection, always spoken of as the "McCoy"
collection, was sold by that gentleman to Mr. W. E. Woodward, whose property it
was, when sold at auction. It consisted almost exclusively of American coins and

medals. It contained, with but one exception, the finest collection of U. S. Cents ever offered at any sale. Exceedingly rich with "Political pieces," many of them exceedingly rare and fine, added to a fine collection of "American Medals," it was deservedly celebrated. To this collection of coins Mr. Woodward added his fine collection of coin catalogues, circulars, pamphlets, and various other " *Numisgraphics.*"

Mr. John F. McCoy, who made this collection of coins, is a native of Pennsylvania, and a prominent leather dealer in "The Swamp," well known among numismatists for his genial, affable, generous disposition; he has dark brown hair, a ruddy complexion, an eye usually beaming with a smile, slightly inclined to be portly in size; he is above the average in height, active in his motions, sociable in conversation, quick in discernment. His tastes early led him to select fine specimens, and judiciously secure a rarity, even if not quite up to his standard, until an opportunity might favor him with a better. He thus became the possessor of one of *the finest* collections in this country of American coins. Not having been so early in the field, as some few others, he, of course, failed to secure some of the rarities; it is much to be regretted that he so early left the numismatic field, where his absence was so undesired.

June 3 | | H. H. Leeds & Co. | N. Y. |
                                      | p. | 1 | 12 | 192 | $4.50

This sale, which consisted principally of books and engravings, had a few medals on pages 11 and 12. The following were the descriptions in the catalogue, to which the prices they sold for, are added.

     ea.,   .18   189.   10 Antique medals of various Persons.
            1.50   190.   1 Fine medal struck, in honor of Jas. Morrison (*sic!*)
     ea.,   .15   190a.   8 Small medals.

O June 21 | George F. Seavey | Bangs, Merwin & Co. | N. Y. |
                                      | p. & n. | 2 | 38 | 831 | $2611.93

This catalogue was issued cut and uncut.

Mr. Geo. F. Seavey was one of those collectors, who devoted their attention almost exclusively to the regular issues of the U. S. Mint, together with the pattern pieces. Quiet and unobstrusive in temperament, like many to be found in New England, yet fixed in his character, he early set a very high standard to be attained in the quality of his collection; this sale comprised only his duplicate coins, with his Washington pieces. His unequalled regular mint series of gold, silver, and copper, he afterwards disposed of, at private sale, to a gentleman in the vicinity of Boston, who at this time probably possesses the finest collection of this series in the United States.

O June 29 | Edward Cogan | Bangs, Merwin & Co. | N. Y. |
                                      | p. & n. | 2 | 32 | 844 | $2524.04

O July 1 | Jacob Harsen and others | Bangs, Merwin & Co. | N. Y. |
                                      | p. & n. | 1 | 14 | 372 | $613.41

Mr. Cogan's catalogue was also issued on large paper.

The latter sale was a continuation of the sale to a third day, on which day the "Addenda" was disposed of ; the collection, belonging to quite a number of different parties, the principal portion belonging, as stated, to Mr. Harsen.

July 13 | J. W. Jacobs | G. W. Beckford & Co. | Boston. | | p. & n. | 1 | 7 | 227 | $85.24

July 13 | J. W. Jacobs | G. W. Beckford & Co. | Boston. | | P. P. | 1 | 7 | 227 | $

July 13 | Addenda | G. W. Beckford & Co. | Boston. | | P. P. & N. | 1 | 1 | 10 | $92.77

The catalogue was also issued subsequently to the sale. In the copy seen, it had only the first twenty-two lots priced. The addenda was sold by manuscript and has since been privately printed; 5 copies on note paper, and twenty on plain paper, with prices and names, with the exception of the last lot, to which only the name of the purchaser is given.

July 27 | George Williams | G. W. Beckford & Co. | Boston. | | p. & n. | 1 | 7 | 236 | $74.31

| Addenda | G. W. Beckford & Co. | Boston. | | P.&N. | 1 | 1 | 11 | $24.08

The addenda was sold from manuscript, and has since been privately printed; 5 copies on note paper, and 20 on plain paper, with prices and names of purchasers.

Aug. 24 | United States | John H. Osgood | Boston. | | | | | | $

This catalogue comprised the cargoes of the prize steamers "Little Ada" and "Ronen," there was but one lot of coin, a lot of American silver half dollars.

Sept. 21 | H. F. Stevens | G. W. Beckford & Co. | Boston. | | p. & n. | 1 | 10 | 305 | $110.86

Oct. 5 | Henry Cook | D. F. McGilvray & Co. | Boston. | | p. & n. | 1 | 16 | 374 | $214.79

Also copies printed on fine paper.

Oct. 18 | W. E. Woodward | G. A. Leavitt | N. Y. | | p. & n. | 5 | 155 | 2942 | $9780.16

This collection was formed principally from the cabinets of the following gentlemen, viz.:

Joseph N. T. Levick,
J. Osborn Emery,
Francis I. Ilsley,
L. H. Abbey,

whose collections had been purchased from them by Mr. Woodward and were here offered combined in one. It is known as Mr. Woodward's fifth sale.

The catalogue was issued cut and uncut, also 15 copies on large paper.

Oct. 19 | | Thomas & Sons | Phia. |
                          | | 1 | 10 | 232 | $

Nov. 16 | Henry Cook | Leonard & Co. | Boston. |
                  | p. & n. | 1 | 8 | 269 | $28.91

    | Addenda | Leonard & Co. | Boston. |
                  | p. & n. | 1 | 4 | 59 | $26.43

    | Supplementary Addenda | Leonard & Co. | Boston. |
                  | P. P. | 1 | 1 | 7 | $5.03

The first addenda is irregularly numbered, there being 5 lots marked 1, and none from 19 to 27. The second or "Supplementary Addenda" was sold from manuscript and has since been privately printed with prices; 5 copies on note paper, and 20 copies on plain paper.

Dec. 14 | | G. W. Beckford & Co. | Boston. |
                  | p. & n. | 1 | 8 | 223 | $

) | S. H. Chadbourne | G. W. Beckford & Co. | Boston. |
                  | p. & n. | 1 | 4 | 99 | $34.06

The lots in the above "Supplement" are numbered from 224 to 322, both inclusive. A supplement was issued after the sales, giving prices and names of purchasers. A few copies of the catalogue were also printed on tinted paper.

Dec. 16 | E. J. Attinelli | Bangs, Merwin & Co. | N. Y. |
                          | | 1 | 16 | 348 | $

The sale was postponed until the 21st.

) Dec. 19 | William C. Prime | Bangs, Merwin & Co. | N. Y. |
                  | p. & n. | 3 | 29 | 1409 | $1112.30

) Dec. 21 | A. J. Carnes | Bangs, Merwin & Co. | N. Y. |
     | Addenda | p. & n. | | 2 | 135 | $251.24

) Dec. 21 | H. Ward and others | Bangs, Merwin & Co. | N. Y. |
     | Addenda | p. & n. | | 4 | 87 | $34.77

Dec. 21 | E. J. Attinelli | Bangs, Merwin & Co. | N. Y. |
     | Addenda | p. & n. | 1 | 16 | 348 | $113.59

The first and second addendas were printed and bound together. Some copies of the third addenda were also bound in with the others, with date of the 16th, changed to that of the 21st. There were also 5 copies of the last addenda, printed on heavy, blue paper, bound in with the catalogue.

1865.

Jan. 10 | Edward M. Thomas | James C. McGuire | Washington. |
                    | | 2 | 43 | 792 | $

In this sale were 383 lots of coins, the remainder books, autographs, etc.

March 6 | | Gilbert & Sampson | Chicago. |
                        | p. | 1 | 14 | 460 | $116.22

This sale comprised coins and continental money.   Many of the lots were
passed and not sold.

The books and papers of the auctioneers, Messrs. Gilbert & Sampson, were
destroyed by the great fire of October 9, 1871.   The firm has since been dissolved.

March 13 | James R. Chilton | Bangs, Merwin & Co. | N. Y. |
                    | p. & n. | 5 | 202 | 3139 | $4150.00

           | Addenda | Bangs, Merwin & Co. | N. Y. |
                    | p. & n. | 1 | 18 | 519 | $297.65

       | Francis S. Edwards | Bangs, Merwin & Co. | N. Y. |
       | Addenda | p. & n. | 1 | 2 | 51 | $89.90

The first addenda belonged to a number of parties; the second, as stated, to
Dr. Francis S. Edwards, which contained some rare and fine pieces.   In this
addenda the lots are distinguished by the letters of the alphabet, first in capitals,
then in small letters, the last lot is described as "A LOT OF SUNDRY PIECES
ALL FINE."   It consisted of 40 pieces.

Dr. Chilton was the well-known chemist, whose fame as such is too far-spread
to render it possible to be added to at this period.   As an antiquarian, his collections of books, coins, casts, etc., bespeak his industry, thought, and care.

March 20 | W. E. Woodward | Cooley & Co. | N. Y. |
                    | p. & n. | 6 | 220 | 3834 | 12,524.66

15 copies on large paper were also issued.
This collection was made up of selections from the cabinet of
              Messrs. Bache.
                    Bertsch,
                    Colin Lightbody,
                    Wm. A. Lilliendahl,
                    Loring Watson.

Chosen from so many fine cabinets, this collection offered a great variety of
coins, ancient, mediæval and modern, coin-catalogues, paper-money, etc.   Mr.
Woodward's sixth sale, so termed.

C March 24 | | M. Thomas & Sons | Phia. |
| | 1 | 12 | 383 | $

April 18 | Mr. Fowler | Joseph Hegeman | Brooklyn. |
| | 1 | 1 | 352 | $0 73

This sheet catalogue offered the following as its only numismatic prize—Lot " 126a valuable Collection of American, Chinese, Russian, Canadian, and French Copper Coins." This valuable collection of 73 pieces brought 73 *cents.*

C April 27 | Joseph N. T. Levick | Bangs, Merwin & Co. | N. Y. |
| | | 41 | 1718 | $

The sale it was thought advisable to postpone, in consequence of the excited state of the entire people, consequent upon the assassination of President Lincoln by Junius B. Booth, who had escaped, but was subsequently captured mortally wounded.

This catalogue was printed and issued in several ways, with and without the part in which was the catalogue-portion of Mr. Levick's collection, also each separately; also, 12 copies of each printed on large paper. Mr. Levick, in consequence of the state of affairs, issued but few copies with the cover bearing the preceeding date, the greater portion of the edition was stripped of its covers and replaced with a new one, bearing the following date, when the sale took place.

May 29 | Joseph N. T. Levick | Bangs, Merwin & Co. | N. Y. |
| | p. & n. | 3 | 41 | 1711 | $2090.03

An explanatory note from Mr. Edward Cogan, and the cover is all the difference between this and the heretofore described catalogue. Attention should have been previously called to the fact that Mr. Levick was the first to issue a catalogue with printed prices immediately after the sale.—See. Dec. 19, 1859.

June 29 | Edward Cogan | Bangs, Merwin & Co. | N. Y. |
| | p. & n. | 1 | 16 | 485 | $869 63

| George B. Mason | Bangs, Merwin & Co. |
| | P. & N. | 1 | 1 | 23 | $18.14

A few copies of the catalogue were issued on large paper. The "Addenda" was sold from manuscript. 20 copies of which have been since privately printed with prices and names.

June 29 | Seth H. Chadbourne | F. J. Sheldon | Providence. |
| | | 9 | 303 | $

Mr. Seth H. Chadbourne was born on the 11th of December, 1836, in the City of Boston, where he still resides. He is a bookkeeper by profession and has been engaged in that capacity with several of the auction-houses in the above named city. A numismatist from inclination, he commenced some twenty years ago the formation, in a modest way, of a cabinet of coins, devoting himself principally to the American series.

Although he has at times disposed of portions of his collection, he still holds on to quite an extensive cabinet of his favorite "Politicals" and "Tradesmen's Tokens." He has long been one of the most active members of the N. E. Numismatic and Archæological Society.

This catalogue has an illustration of a Massachusetts shilling on the first page. The sale did not take place. the collection was withdrawn and sold in Boston.

July 12 | S. H. Chadbourne | D. F. McGilvray & Co. | Boston.|
 | p. & n. | 1 | 9 | 303 | $60.81

This is the same collection and catalogue as the preceeding. The name of the auctioneers, date of sale, etc., being printed on a slip and pasted over the name of Mr. Sheldon. etc.

Oct. 16 | Francis S. Edwards | Bangs, Merwin & Co. | N. Y. |
 | p. & n. | 5 | 101 | 2907 | $4677.83

Oct. 20| M. L. Babcock and others | Bangs, Merwin & Co.|N.Y.|
 | Addenda | p. & n. | 1 | 1 | 24 | $32.09

Dr. Francis S. Edwards, whose decease brought his large and valuable collection under the hammer, was an Englishman by birth, by profession a physician. To him was attributed the appearance of several counterfeit pieces of rare American coins and medals, which, though extremely well executed, were quickly detected. The coins in the addenda belonged principally to Mr. Babcock and the estate of Dr. Chilton.

Oct. 24 | J. E. Dawley | Bangs, Merwin & Co. | N. Y. |
 | p. & n. | 2 | 52 | 1169 | $553.59

Oct. 26 | Dr. John J. Abrahams | Samuel Hatch | Boston. |
 | p. & n. | 1 | 1 | 173 | $164.96

The books and papers of Mr. Hatch were all destroyed in the great fire in 1872.

Nov. 13 | Benj. Haines & J. H. Griscom | Cooley & Co.|N. Y.|
 | p. & n. | 3 | 51 | 1444 | $515.81

This sale consisted largely of autographs and continental money.

Dec. 19 | W. E. Woodward | Geo. A. Leavitt | N. Y. |
 | p. & n. | 5 | 109 | 2678 | $4251.06

Oct. 22 | A. S. Robinson | Geo. A. Leavitt | N. Y. |
 | Addenda | p. & n. | 1 | 4 | 100 | $64.17

Fifteen copies of this catalogue were issued on large paper.

The collection was formed, as stated in the title page of the catalogue "from the cabinets of Messrs. Bache, Bertsch, Colburn, Emery, Finotti, Ilsley, Levick,

Lilliendahl, Lightbody, McCoy, Semple, Shurtleff, and other collections. The addenda, which belonged to Mr. Robinson, bears no date. This is known as Mr. Woodward's seventh sale.

Dec. 23 | S. H. Chadbourne *et.al.* | Conant & Sherburne | Boston. |
| p. | | | 1 | 208 | $28.44

This catalogue was also issued on dark, tinted paper.

This sale, I am informed, "was got up for *fun* alone, by myself and several friends, every lot was sold and paid for." The bidders assumed the names of the leading numismatists of the country.

Dec. 27 | | Bangs, Merwin & Co. | N. Y. |
| | | | 5 | 114 | $

On page 5 of this catalogue, lots 101 @ 105 inclusive, are medals. The collection was not sold.

1866.

Feb. 14 | Dr. T. Larkin Turner | Samuel Hatch | Boston. |
| p. | 2 | 22 | 841 | $208.59

o | F. E. Coffin | Samuel Hatch | Boston. |
| p. | 1 | 1 | 81 | $18.49

The latter of the above is an addenda.

Feb. 19 | E. I. Barra | L. Keller | San Francisco. |
| | 2 | 24 | 519 | $

Probably the first coin sale on the Pacific Coast.

Feb. 27 | Robert B. Chambers | Geo. A. Leavitt | N. Y. |
| p. & n. | 3 | 71 | 1745 | $1431.40

This collection was catalogued by Mr. Woodward, and sold under his supervision, but did not belong to him.

March 6 | | Birch & Sons | Phia. |
| p. | 2 | 15 | 429 | $

March 26 | | Bangs, Merwin & Co. | N. Y. |
| p. | 1 | 13 | 307 | $0.74

This was a book sale, in which was the following described lot:
"307, 37 pieces of Old Copper and Brass Coins," sold at 2 cents each.

⌐ April 16 | A. C. Kline | Birch & Sons | Phia. |
                                 | | 2 | 18 | 690 | $

673 lots are numbered, and 17 are not.

○ April.24 | Francis S. Hoffman | Leavitt, Strebeigh & Co. | N.Y. |
                          | p. & n. | 4 | 120 | 2340 | $3331.79

This was a collection belonging to Mr. Woodward at the time of the auction,
being known as his eighth semi-annual sale.
There were 15 copies issued on large paper.

① May 2 | Edward Cogan | Birch & Sons | Phia. |
                          | p. & n. | 1 | 10 | 338 | $190.70

By an error, the catalogue is dated the 3d, the sale took place on Wednesday,
May 2d.   A few copies printed on fine paper.

② May 23 | Henry M. Brooks | Leonard & Co. | Boston |
                          | p. & n. | 2 | 25 | 582 | $304.43

⊘ May 24 | Rev. James Eddy | Leonard & Co. | Boston |
                          | p. & n. | 1 | 11 | 263 | $268.82

The sales comprised books, coins, and autographs.   A few copies of the catalogue were issued, printed on fine paper.

          26 | Oscar H. Harpel | S. G. Hubbard | Cinn. |
                          | p. | 1 | 1 | 270 | $

This is a broadside sheet, principally books, 28 lots of coins are offered.

⊘ Oct. 18 | J. Rosenthal | Miner & Somerville | N. Y. |
                          | p. & n. | 1 | 14 | 251 | $318.67

189 lots were sold; the remainder were withdrawn, the owner being dissatisfied
with the prices, which those sold brought.   Catalogued by Geo. B. Mason.

○ Oct. 19 | J. M. R. Story | Samuel Hatch | Boston |
                          | p. & n. | 1 | 14 | 436 | $268.12

A few copies were also issued, printed on tinted paper.

      Oct. 24 | Pawner's Bank | D. F. McGilvray & Co. | Boston |
                          | | 1 | 16 | 553 | $

Twelfth semi-annual sale.   The lots are not numbered consecutively, but
apparently by the numbers placed upon the articles when pledged in pawn, "on
Page 13 are 21 pieces of Silver."
   The catalogue does not state whether these were a portion of those received by
Judas Iscariot, and on Page 14, "No. 40,839," is a watch, coins, chain, and key.

Nov. 9 | Dr. G. T. Collins | S. G. Hubbard | Cinn. |
                        | p. | 1 | 1 | 263 | $210.70

A broadside sheet with 209 lots of coins ; the remainder, books, etc.

○ Nov. 13 | Wm. H. Corner | Leavitt, Strebeigh & Co. | N. Y. |
                        | | 143 | 1735 | $30.25

This was a collection of books, autographs, engravings, and the following
described lot of coins, on page 137, lot:
   " 1655.—A collection of 45 Washington coins and medals, including many
      rare pieces in silver, bronze, copper, and white metal; one believed
      to be unique; mostly in very fine condition."

Nov. 27 , | Thomas & Sons | Phia. |
                        | p. & n. | 1 | 10 | 366 | $

₵ Dec. 6 | Colin Lightbody | Bangs, Merwin & Co. | N. Y. |
                        | p. & n. | 2 | 38 | 774 | $3731.83

An interesting catalogue.   Mr. Lightbody was by occupation a plumber in
this city.   An enthusiastic seeker after fine and rare pieces; that he was quite
successful, the high average, brought by his collection, amply proves.

₯ Dec. 10 | Jencks & Paine | Leavitt, Strebeigh & Co. | N. Y. |
                   · | p. & n. | 3 | 86 | 2163 | $1525.93

Messrs. A. V. Jencks and G. T. Paine, who were the owners of the above collection, are both residents of Rhode Island and well known numismatists.

Dec. 15 | | Miner & Somerville | N. Y. |
                        | | 1 | 8 | 130 | $00.86

There are no coins in this catalogue, as printed, but the following coins were
sold as a star lot. viz. :
   "A set of United States cents;" Commencing at 1800.   57 pieces "sold
      @ 1½ cts each."

○ Dec. 18 | Henry M. Brooks | Leonard & Co. | Boston |
                        | p. | 1 | 17 | 349 | $

This collection, principally of books, yet comprised a little of almost everything.   Lots 288 to 311 on page 15 are "Coin and Medals.   All very fine."

1867.

Jan. 11 | Bernard McGuire | Bangs, Merwin & Co. | N. Y. |
| p. & n. | 1 | 12 | 307 | $126.55

This sale was principally books. The following was the only lot of coins:
"155. Five thousand Copper and Brass Coins. Many of them scarce, curious, and rare."
Instead of being but 5,000 there were 10,770 pieces, which were sold to Mr. Cogan @ $1.17½ cents per hundred.

Jan. 16 | Walter Deakin | D. Scott & Co. | Chicago |
| p. & n. | 1 | 15 | 541 | $

March 5 | Walter Deakin | D. Scott & Co. | Chicago |
| p. & n. | 1 | 4 | 347 | $61.87

March 18 | | Bangs, Merwin & Co. | N. Y. |
| p. | 1 | 8 | 218 | $42.74

This sale comprised 91 lots of autographs, and 127 lots of coins.

March 18 | | T. Birch & Son | Phia. |
| p. | 1 | 11 | 388 | $551.57

March 19 | | B. Scott, Jr. | Phia. |
| p. & n. | 1 | 16 | 350 | $159.74

Mr. Scott can give no information, relative to this sale.

March 22 | | Bangs, Merwin & Co. | N. Y. |
| | | 1 | 162 | $

This sale was postponed to the 27th, when the same sheet-catalogue was used.

March 27 | | Bangs, Merwin & Co. | N. Y. |
| | 1 | 1 | 162 | $

Lot 115 is a "Medallion, Bronze", it was not sold.

April 18 | | S. G. Hubbard | Cinn. |
| | 3 | 57 | 946 | $

This sale was nearly all books, but the last lot is described as follows :
"946. A Lot of Copper coins Sutler's Checks, Store Cards, etc."

① April 18 | W. E. Woodward | Leavitt, Strebeigh & Co.| N. Y.|
| p. & n. | 3 | 72 | 1647 | $1740.90

April 19 | | Leavitt, Strebeigh & Co. | N. Y. |
| p. & n. | 1 | 4 | 68 | $164.96

The latter was an "Additional Catalogue." It is probably needless to say that almost every one of Mr. Woodward's catalogues are well worthy the time spent in reading and comparing them. This was Mr. Woodward's ninth semi-annual sale.

⓪ April 24 | Zanoni & Bogert | Bangs, Merwin & Co. | N. Y. |
| p. & n. | 3 | 41 | 1129 | $2651.29

Messrs. Joseph Zanoni of Cincinnati and Henry Bogert of New York, were the owners of the above fine collection.

June 5 | | Leonard & Co. | Boston |
| p. | 1 | 6 | 304 | $40.00

| Addenda | Leonard & Co. | Boston |
| P. & N. | 1 | 1 | 7 | $43.61

This sale consisted principally of autographs; the last 52 lots only of the catalogue being coins.

The addenda was sold from manuscript, and 20 copies have since been privately printed.

○ June 5 | L. Brechemin | Davis & Harvey | Phia. |
| p. | 3 | 40 | 1309 | $

June 13 | | Bangs, Merwin & Co. | N. Y. |
| p. | 1 | 16 | 334 | $11.38

In this catalogue of books, engravings, etc., lot 332 was a "Set of American cents from 1793 to 1867," the latter date should have been printed correctly 1857. The lot sold for 17½ cents each.

○ June 27 | J. K. Curtis | Bangs, Merwin & Co. | N. Y. |
| | 2 | 16 | 494 | $00.55

No. 464 in this catalogue is a lot of Chinese coins, sold for 55 cents.

July 8 | | Putnam Bros. | Worcester |
| | | 40 | 904 | $

Principally books. Forty-four of the lots are unnumbered. Following lot 864 is a lot, described as follows :

"Magic lantern and slides. Also a small collection of Engravings, Medals, Relics, &c." [Worcester, Mass.]

○ Sept. 25 | S. H. Chadbourne | Samuel Hatch | Boston |
                                | p. & n. | 1 | 28 | 769 | $330.68

⌒ Sept. 30 | Merrit & Mauterstock | Bangs, Merwin & Co. | N.Y. |
        \ | p. & n. | 1 | 20 | 564 | $1110.09

Sept. 30 | Addenda | Bangs, Merwin & Co. | N. Y. |
                                | P. & N. | 1 | 1 | 12 | $28.75

The collection belonged to Messrs. George S. Merrit and Joseph W. Mauterstock. The addenda to several parties; the various lots are distinguished by letters. This addenda was sold from manuscript and 20 copies have since been privately printed.

Oct. 15 | | T. Birch & Son | Phia. |
                                | p. & n. | 1 | 12 | 534 | $

Oct. | | Samuel Hatch | Boston |
                        | P. | 1 | 2 | 95 | $6.87

This collection was sold between the 15th and the 25th from ms., of which 25 copies have been since printed; 12 of which are on note paper.

⌢ Oct. 22 | Alfred S. Robinson | Leavitt, Strebeigh & Co. | N.Y. |
                        | | | 1 | 33 | $

See addenda to Mickley sale.

⌒ Oct. 23 | Pawner's Bank | D. F. McGilvray & Co. | Boston |
                        | | 1 | 18 | 770 | $

[Fourteenth sale.] The lots are numbered probably in the order in which they were pawned.
The following lots are described on the respective pages:
        Page 11.   Lot   268   "2 Silver Medals."
        Page 13.   "   1089   "2 Silver Medals."
        Page 14.   " 41,196   "1 Bag Cents."

Oct. 24 | | M. Thomas & Son | Phia. |
                        | | 1 | 1 | 262 | $

This is a large sheet-catalogue; the lots not numbered; the last 19 lots are gold, silver, and copper coins, 179 pieces.

Oct. 28 | Joseph J. Mickley | Leavitt, Strebeigh & Co. | N. Y. |
                        | p. & n. | 5 | 196 | 3349 | $13,285.70

Oct. 22 | Alfred S. Robinson|Leavitt, Strebeigh & Co.|N. Y.|
        | Addenda | p. & n. | 1 | 1 | 33 | $22.37

60 copies of the above catalogue were printed "on extra heavy tinted paper.'
The addenda belonged to Mr. Robinson, is printed on a long slip, and bears the
date of the 22d, but was sold subsequent to the Mickley Collection.

The above celebrated collection was the property of Mr. W. E. Woodward when
placed before the public for competition. His tenth semi-annual sale.

Mr. Mickley is a native of Pennsylvania, where he was born March, 24, 1799.
Probably every numismatist knows that it was his attempt to procure a cent of
that year that led him into the formation of a collection, which was almost unrivalled, both in its fineness and extent, as also in the rarity of many of the pieces
it contained. Mr. Mickley was justly proud of his cabinet and ever ready to exhibit
it to numismatists, with a courtesy and urbanity which became proverbial. The
reputation of the collection becoming generally known, tempted ignorant scoun-
drels, who knew not that its value consisted not so much in its value as bullion, as
in the condition and rarity of the coins; a burglary was the result; Mr. Mickley's
store being on the night of the 13th April, 1867, broken into, and robbed of a
part of the foreign portion of the collection to the value of about $2000. For-
tunately for American Numismatology, the coins of this country escaped their
notice and vandalism. This event undoubtedly produced a feeling of insecurity
which, at Mr. Mickley's advancing age, induced him to at once dispose of the
cherished objects of his solicitude and care, the labor and search of many years
spent in gathering together these mementoes of the past.

The gem of the collection was the 1804 Dollar, which was bought by Mr. William
A. Lilliendahl for $750. Probably the highest sum ever paid in this country for
a single coin.

Nov. 12 | Louis Borg | H. H. Leeds & Co. | N. Y. |
        | | | 56 | 490 | $

This catalogue comprised Mr. Borg's collection of medals, but a few lots of
which were put up and bid in, the remainder were withdrawn; the prices offered
not being satisfactory. The medals are extensively described.

Nov. 12 | Louis Borg | H. H. Leeds & Co. | N. Y. |
        | | | 32 | 1061 | $

This catalogue comprised Mr. Borg's coins. The collection was withdrawn for
reasons alluded to in connection with his collection of medals.

Mr. Borg was for many years the Consul of France in New York. A gentleman
of culture and refined tastes, whose affection for his coins gave them greater value
in his estimation than they would bring before a less appreciative public.

There were other separate catalogues comprising furniture, paintings, etc., but,
as they contain no coins, are not otherwise referred to.

Nov. 27 | | Thomas & Sons | Phia. |
        | | 1 | 10 | 366 | $

Dec. 27 | | Bangs, Merwin & Co. | N. Y. |
                                   | | 1 | 8 | 181 | $

On page 10, Lot 29, is described as "Medallions, Bronze in black Walnut frame"; it sold for 15 cents.   This lot was neither coins nor medals, but electrotype shells, and should not have been classed among coin-catalogues, but that some one hereafter, not knowing the facts, might imagine he had discovered a "mare's nest."   The following is another example.

Dec. 30 | | Bangs, Merwin & Co. | N. Y. |
                                   | | 1 | 8 | 181 | $

On pages 7 and 8 are described the following:
     "10 French Medallions Head of W. H. Seward."
     "10   "   "   "   "   "   with gilt rim."
     "10   "   "   "   Napoleon III."
     "10   "   "   "   Empress Eugenie."
     " 8 French Medallions Prince Albert."
     " 6   "   "   Richard Cobden."

1868.

May 13 | | Leonard & Co. | Boston |
                                   | p. & n. | 1 | 7 | 453 | $313.78

June 3 | James Oliver | Bangs, Merwin & Co. | N. Y. |
                                   | p. & n. | 3 | 38 | 1456 | $1232.61

Mr. Oliver was among the earliest coin-collectors in this city, for a long time Secretary of the "American Numismatic and Archæological Society" of New York; consequently too well and favorably known among collectors, to require further notice here.

July 1 | John C. Nippes | T. Birch & Son | Phia. |
                                   | p. & n. | 2 | 23 | 644 | $

Oct. 28 | J. C. Randall | T. Birch & Son | Phia. |
                                   | p. & n. | 2 | 28 | 883 | $1294.45

Nov. 5 | | S. Hatch & Co. | Boston |
                                   | P. | 1 | 2 | 53 | $45.34

This collection was sold from manuscript.   It has since been privately printed. (25 Copies.)

Nov. 28 | John McLane | Bangs, Merwin & Co. | N. Y. |
                                   | p. & n. | 1 | 13 | 252 | $25.26

| Addenda | Bangs. Merwin & Co. | N. Y. |
| P. & N. | 1 | 1 | 4 | $1.39

There were but 11 lots of coins in the catalogue, which brought the above stated sum. The addenda was sold from manuscript, but 20 copies of it have been since privately printed.

Dec. 14 | J. de F. Burns *et al.*|Leavitt, Strebeigh & Co.|N. Y.|
| p. & n. | 2 | 53 | 1526 | $90.83

This collection consisted very largely of books. The entire collection bringing nearly $1300.

1869.

April 13 | E. J. Farmer | T. Birch & Son | Phia. |
| p. & n. | 3 | 36 | 950 | $1450.53

April 16 | | Leonard & Co. | Boston |
| | 1 | 4 | 189 | $

The perspicuity of this catalogue may be readily understood from the following sentence, which appears on the last page. "Note. A full explanation will be given of the whole list, as every coin is named in manuscript list but confused in the abridgement for catalogue. J. L."

May 31 | George B. Davis | Bangs, Merwin & Co. | N. Y. |
| p. & n. | 1 | 18 | 459 | $486.37

This collection consisted very largely of store cards and rebellion tokens, or "copperheads," issued during the rebellion of 1861—65.

June 4 | Tudor & Parker | Leavitt, Strebeigh & Co. | N. Y. |
| p. & n. | 2 | 53 | 1179 | $134.90

This collection belonged to Mr. Tudor and Mr. W. A. Parker.

June 5 | J. J. Taylor | Leavitt, Strebeigh & Co. | N. Y. |
| p. & n. | 1 | 1 | 7 | $4.48

There were 819 lots of autographs, minerals, etc., also, 360 lots of coins; the entire collection bringing nearly $1000. There was an addenda sold from manuscript, the first lot only being coins. This has been since privately printed 5 copies on note, and 20 on plain paper.

June 9 | Dr. W. W. Morgan | T. Birch & Son | Phia. |
| p. & n. | 2 | 40 | 1137 | $

This might appropriately be termed a "Museum Catalogue," comprising as it does, curiosities and rarities from each of the three great kingdoms, Animal, Vegetable, and Mineral; ancient and modern: written and unwritten. The last 100 lots are incorrectly numbered, an 0 being substituted for a 1.

June 23 | M. L. Mackenzie | Leavitt, Strebeigh & Co. | N. Y. |
| p. & n. | 2 | 56 | 770 | $4430.51

June 23 | M. L. Mackenzie | Leavitt, Strebeigh & Co. | N. Y. |
5 plates of photographs.

June 23 | M. L. Mackenzie | Leavitt, Strebeigh & Co. | N. Y. |
4 plates of photographs.

June 23 | M. L. Mackenzie | Leavitt, Strebeigh & Co. | N. Y. |
Large paper.

The sale of this celebrated collection, noted for the superior quality of the
pieces offered therein, for which the aggregate amount, paid for the number of
lots, forms a good criterion; being an average of nearly six dollars a lot, extremely
few lots consisting of more than one piece; gold forming the least part of the
value.   The set of U. S. Cents being the finest ever offered in any one collection.
The catalogues were issued with and without photographs, some with five, and
others with four plates.   A few copies were also issued on large paper.   The early
death of Mr. Mackenzie was an event most deeply regretted by numismatists
generally, and most particularly by those of this city.

June 28 | Wm. H. Corner | Leavitt, Strebeigh & Co. | N. Y. |
| p. | 3 | 82 | 1177 | $0 50

This was a book-sale, but on page 63 there is one lot described as follows:
"Five pieces money in Circulation in Philadelphia during the War of
1812—15."   Sold to H. for 50 cents.

June 30 | M. W. Dickeson | T. Birch & Son | Phia. |
| p. | 1 | 8 | 205 | $

This collection was almost exclusively American pieces, consisting principally
of cents and half cents in large quantities.

July 29 | M. W. Dickeson | T. Birch & Son | Phia. |
| p. | 1 | 8 | 272 | $521.13

Many of the coins in this catalogue were in large lots. but quite a number were
rare and valuable.

Sept. 6 | Edward P. Thorn | T. Birch & Son | Phia. |
| p. | 3 | 35 | 1000 | $980.66

Sept. 27 | Alfred B. Taylor | Bangs. Merwin & Co. | N. Y. |
| p. & n. | 2 | 46 | 967 | $2375.58

— Oct. 13 | M. W. Dickeson | | T. Birch & Son | Phia.
| p. & n. | 2 | 26 | 735 | $

This is a catalogue of curiosities and, like a couple of other catalogues previously described, should not justly be styled a "Coin Catalogue." It contains "Colonial moneys," but not a coin; the nearest approach to one, being lot 193, described as a "Chinese Coin Mould, brass." Then why include it in the list? Solely, to object to its being called a "Coin Catalogue!"

Oct. 15 | A. S. Robinson | Bangs, Merwin & Co. | N. Y. |
| p. & n. | 1 | 20 | 494 | $448.33

o Oct. 18 | J. Colvin Randall | Bangs, Merwin & Co. | N. Y. |
| p. & n. | 2 | 34 | 665 | $1843.89

A few copies of this catalogue, six in number, it is said, were issued on large paper.

Nov. 16 | John W. Haseltine | Bangs, Merwin & Co. | N. Y. |
| p. & n. | 2 | 42 | 968 | $1377.62

There was an additional lot of "1 Granby Copper," sold to Mr. Randall for $25.00.

John W. Haseltine, the owner of this collection, who has since become so well known to the numismatists of this country as a prominent dealer in coins, was born on the 6th of September, 1838, in the City of Philadelphia, where he was educated. At the age of sixteen he became a clerk in the book-trade, subsequently was engaged in the wholesale boot and shoe business. In 1861, when th rebellion broke out, he was in New Orleans; hastening North, he assisted in raising a company, of which he became First Lieutenant, was afterwards promoted to be Captain in the Second Pennsylvania Cavalry, which was under the command of Col. R. Butler Price, mustered in the U. S. Service, in October, 1861, serving with his regiment in all the battles in which it was engaged, and received several slight wounds; but at Deep Bottom, near Richmond, Va., on the 16th of August, 1864, he was again wounded, so severely as to necessitate his being brought home. He was subsequently employed as secretary and treasurer of several mining companies; while thus employed, he sold his collection. He was the special partner of E. Mason, Jr., in the firm of Mason & Co. This partnership not proving a successful venture, he afterwards devoted his entire attention to the coin and curiosity business, on his sole account, in which he has brought out from their secret repositories, a number of scarce and rare pieces, among which may be enumerated the unique Nova Constellatio Dollar, and half Dollar, the former property of Charles Thomson, secretary of the first continental congress, also, the unique Washington cent, with reverse of the New Jersey cent.

Mr. Haseltine is also the author and compiler of an illustrated descriptive list of the colonial and continental paper money, as also of a descriptive catalogue of the confederate paper money.

In his coin sale catalogues, Mr. Haseltine seldom, if ever, overrates, and more frequently underrates the quality of the pieces he describes, and still more frequently makes no mention of their quality or rarity, possibly from a mistaken idea, that every body else knows more on that subject than himself, or from a determination to keep on the safe side. The same trait of conscientiousness, highly to his credit, will probably have been observed, that, in buying, he endeavors to purchase for his patron at the lowest possible price, regardless of the sum to which he may be authorized to advance.

Nov. 17 | Charles S. Fellows | Leonard, Bird & Co. | Boston|
| p. | 1 | 16 | 727 | $319.22

| Addenda | Leonard, Bird & Co. | Boston |
| p. | 1 | 1 | 11 | $

The title and business of the above-named auction house, is now Henry C. Bird & Co., No. 146 Tremont Street, Boston. The "addenda," which has been printed since the sale, gives the division of lot 295½ into the 11 lots, made by selling the proof sets of each year separate.

Nov. 25 | G. W. Jacobs | Bangs, Merwin & Co. | N. Y. |
| p. & n. | 1 | 18 | 789 | $535.69

Nov. 26 | | Bangs, Merwin & Co. | N. Y. |
| p. & n. | 1 | 14 | 276 | $2.50

In this catalogue are described the following lots, viz.:
      "186. Card containing about 75 shinplasters of 1862. Framed."
      "187. 2 Cards of Photographs of National and United States Treasury
      Notes, and Old Coins."
The first lot sold for $2.00, and the next @ 25 cents each.

Nov. 29 | John Bartram | Martin Bros | Phia. |
| p. & n. | 2 | 31 | 853 | $

Dec. 1 | M. W. Dickeson | T. Birch & Son | Phia.—
| p. | 1 | 16 | 511 | $

Coins, books and curiosities.

Dec. 17 | J. M. Wilbur | Bangs, Merwin & Co. | N. Y. |
| p. & n. | 2 | 25 | 1958 | $329.51

This interesting collection, in which such terms as the following, are of frequent occurrence, "poor," "poorer," "worse," "extremely poor," "unusually poor," "wretchedly poor," "still worse," "exceedingly poor," "poorer still." But. "poor" Mr. Cogan, who catalogued the collection, nevertheless, did not succeed. I believe, in getting down to "the poorest." What could have been the object of cataloguing sixty cents of one date (1847) in as many consecutive lines, the best one of which was classed as "barely fair?" the same term being the most favorable one, used for over 300 lots, which were sold at one cent each, if the catalogue before me is correctly priced.

Dèc. 21 | | Martin Bros. | Phia. |
| p. | 1 | 26 | 622 | $

Dèc. 22 | M. W. Dickeson | T. Birch & Son | Phia. |
| p. | 1 | 12 | 422 | $

Another collection of coins, curiosities, and coin books.

1870.

☉ Jàn. 21 | James B. Longacre | M. Thomas & Sons | Phia. |
| p. & n. | 1 | 28 | 632 | $948.64

☽ | Addenda | M. Thomas & Sons | Phia. |
| p. & n. | 1 | 1 | 33 | $32.87

Though containing a large number of pattern pieces, yet it is not so full as might have been expected from one so long connected with the U. S. Mint.

April 12 | | T. Birch & Son | Phia. |
| p. & n. | 1 | 16 | 336 | $

These catalogues are all printed in fine style on large paper.

☿ April 22 | Edward Cogan | Bangs, Merwin & Co. | N. Y. |
| p. & n. | 1 | 22 |·556 | $459.47

| Addenda | Bangs, Merwin & Co. | N. Y. |
| P. & N. | 1 | 1 | 4 | $1.05

The addenda was sold from manuscript, 20 copies have been since privately printed.

♄ April 28 | F. P. Maguire | Leavitt, Strebeigh & Co. | N. Y. |
| p. & n. | 2 | 39 | 391 | $655.44

♇ April 29 | A. S. Robinson | Leavitt, Strebeigh & Co. | N. Y.|
| p. & n. | 1 | 3 | 49 | $10.50

The catalogue of this collection, "BELONGING TO A WELL-KNOWN CON-NOISSEUR," was issued in good style, being the one known as the "Tinfoil Covers." The latter sale was an addenda.

May 3 | L. Montgomery Bond | Leavitt, Strebeigh & Co. | N.Y. |
p. & n. | 3 | 123 | 1406 | $68.04

⟨ | Fragment | Leavitt, Strebeigh & Co. | N. Y. |
| p. & n. | 1 | 16 | 272 | $68.04

This collection consisted principally of books, but included coins as well as
autographs, etc, issued in fine style on tinted paper. The "fragment" or separate
portion of the catalogue, comprises that portion of the collection contained from
lot 1135 to 1406. both inclusive, and is that portion which has a list of the coins.
which latter brought $68.04. Photographs of the medal. lot 1404, were issued
separately at 25 cents each. This medal was put up on the condition that a starting
bid should be made of $4000.00; no one appearing to be disposed to so start it, it
was withdrawn.

○ May 19 | M. W. Dickeson | T. Birch & Son | Phia. |
| p. & n. | 1 | 15 | 448 | $

① May 25 | J. C. Newcomb | Leavitt. Strebeigh & Co. | N.Y. |
| p. & n. | 3 | 107 | 928 | $2520.74

ν The same illustrated with eight plates of photographs.
This is another elegantly printed catalogue on fine paper. A portion of the
collection was formerly the property of that eminent antiquarian, Mr. John Allan.
The hand of the distinguished numismatist, the President of the "Numismatic
and Archæogical Society" may be recognized in the description of a number of
the pieces. And the whole does credit to Mr. Cogan. who had the management.

© June 17 | Francis Smith | Bangs, Merwin & Co. | N. Y. |
| p. & n. | 1 | 16 | 226 | $146.04

June 17 | Francis Smith | Bangs, Merwin & Co. | N. Y. |
| p. & n. | 1 | 11 | 167 | $66.87

⟨ June 17 | | Leavitt, Strebeigh & Co. | N.Y. |
| p. & n. | 1 | 31 | 601 | $1204.25

        The same with plates.

① Oct. 4 | William Fewsmith | Leavitt, Strebeigh & Co. | N.Y. |
| p. & n. | 4 | 102 | 2501 | $4746.44

○ Oct. 19 | J. W. Kline | Bangs, Merwin & Co. | N. Y. |
| p. & n. | 1 | 18 | 378 | $333.53

○ Dec. 8 | W. S. Lincoln & Son | Leonard & Co. | Boston |
| | | 32 | 991 | $

This sale was postponed to December 22.

Dec. 20 | | Leavitt, Strebeigh & Co. | N. Y. |
| p. | 1 | 30 | 188 | $30.00

Lot 69 in this collection of books, etc., is described as follows:
"France. Series of Medals, Busts of the Kings of France, from Pharamond, including two symbolic heads for the two Republics of 1792 and 1848. In all seventy-five Bronze Medals, size 33 American coin scale, in neat velvet lined red morocco box. Capital impressions in perfect order."

○ Dec. 21 | William Idler | Leavitt, Strebeigh & Co. | N. Y. |
| p. & n. | 1 | 20 | 405 | $507.27

Dec. 21 | M. W. Dickeson | T. Birch & Son | Phia. |
| | 1 | 1 | 270 | $

This is a large sheet-catalogue; the first 52 lots being books, minerals and curiosities, the remainder coins.

○ Dec. 22 | W. S. Lincoln & Son | Leonard & Co. | Boston |
| p. & n. | 2 | 32 | 991 | $1282.11

○ | Addenda | Leonard & Co. | Boston |
| p. | 1 | 1 | 24 | $23.96

This collection was sent to this country by the well-known London firm of coin-dealers.

Dec. 28 | M. W. Dickeson | T. Birch & Son | Phia. |
| | 1 | 1 | 293 | $

Another broadside catalogue of "sundries," belonging to the same owner, as the collection sold by the same firm, on the 21st.
The first 100 lots are minerals, books, and other curiosities, then follow the coins.

1871.

Jan. 11 | M. W. Dickeson | T. Birch & Son | Phia. |
                             | | 1 | 1 | 273 | $

A broadside sheet.   107 lots of books, curiosities, etc.; the remainder coins.

Jan. 12 | | Leonard & Co. | Boston. |
                             | | 1 | 19 | 214 | $

This collection comprised principally paintings, with some 77 lots of coins.

Jan. 16 | Cogan & Halliwell | Bangs, Merwin & Co. | N. Y. |
                             | p. & n. | 1 | 22 | 499 | $588.12

There was an additional lot sold, being an 1836 dollar, purchased by Mr. Brown
for $6.00. The collection, comprised in the catalogue, belonged to Messrs. Edward
Cogan and J. R. Halliwell.

Feb. 16 | Mason & Co. | Leavitt, Strebeigh & Co. | N. Y. |
                             | p. & n. | 2 | 37 | 858 | $1095.15

(D) Feb. 27 | William F. Packer | Bangs, Merwin & Co. | N. Y. |
                             | p. & n. | 5 | 106 | 3018 | $5888.16

This collection, the former property of the late Governor Packer of Pennsylvania, (who died September 27th, 1870,) was one of the finest ever offered; comprising, as it did, ancient and modern coins, it also presented a large representation
from almost every country on the globe.

March 29 | M. W. Dickeson | T. Birch & Son | Phia. |
                             | | 1 | 1 | 309 | $

A broadside sheet-catalogue of books, curiosities, and coins.

(D) April 3 | Bangs, Merwin & Co. | N. Y. |
                             | p. & n. | 3 | 73 | 1758 | $2573.79

The same uncut.
The same with illustrations.
This collection, generally known as the "Montreal" or "Canada" collection,
was sold through Mr. Cogan. The work of cataloguing the coins is attributed to
Mr. A. Sandham, of Montreal, who was probably the owner.

April 8 | J. W. Kline | Bangs, Merwin & Co. | N. Y. |
                             | p. & n. | 1 | 1 | 310 | $180.52

A broadside sheet.

(April 13 | J. W. Kline | G. A. Leavitt & Co. | N. Y. |
                                | | | 11 | 300 | $

The sale of this collection was postponed to the 21st, the same catalogue being
used, the change of date being made by a pen or pencil.

O April 14 | George P. Upton | W. A. Butters & Co.|Chicago|
                               | p. | 1 | 15 | 240 | $358.77

o April 21 | J. W. Kline | G. A. Leavitt & Co. | N. Y. |
                                | p. & n. | 1 | 11 | 300 | $300.29

This catalogue is the same as that of the 13th, the change of date being made
with a pen.

April 25 | Chas. W. Frederickson|Bangs, Merwin & Co.|N.Y.|
                                | p. | 3 | 45 | 744 | $0.50

Lot 718 must have felt among uncongenial spirits, and probably sadly taxed at
times with overwork, being alone among so many books.   The following is the
description :
  "MYSTICAL COIN. Keeps off. Evil Spirits, etc. — From Judge Furman's
Collection with MS."   Mr. Haseltine became the purchaser at 50 cents.

: May 3 | Emil Cauffmann | Bangs, Merwin & Co. | N. Y. |
                                | p. & n. | 3 | 40 | 903 | $1789.52

  ' The same uncut.
  ' The same with illustrations.
  A supplement, giving "List of Prices," was shortly after the sale published
under the broad seal of the "N. E. Numismatic & Archæological Society," which
seal is embellished, in addition to the above inscription, with a large and broad
band, on which are displayed some comical looking figures, between which are
the abbreviations of the names of the New England States.   In the field is a large
half starved and evidently puzzled sphinx couchant, looking hungrily at a couple
of palm-trees, which he holds between his paws, his tail gracefully swinging; the
swaying of the tail threatening to demolish the apex of a pyramid in the vicinity.

May 24 | Henry W. Poole | Leonard & Co. | Boston. |
                                | | 3 | 62 | 1009 | $

June 1 | Benj. Betts | Bangs, Merwin & Co. | N. Y. |
                                | p. & n. | 2 | 45 | 904 | $1663.83

June 2 | Addenda | Bangs, Merwin & Co. | N. Y. |
                             | P.&N. | 1 | 1 | 3 | $5.08

The "addenda" was sold from manuscript, and an edition of 20 copies has been since privately printed. The "N. E. Numismatic & Archaeological Society" issued soon after the sale a "List of Prices," being their second issue of this character.

ɔ June 12 | J. W. Kline | Bangs, Merwin & Co. | N. Y. |
                             | p. & n. | 1 | 1 | 34? | $238.78

A broadside sheet.   Coins, relics, and curiosities.

Mr. John W. Kline, the owner of the above collection is one of the early collectors of this country, not making coins a specialty, but devotes his attention as well to Mineralogy, Conchology and Philately, as also to the undefineable genus known as curiosities, in all of which he has for quite a number of years been well known as an extensive dealer.

Mr. Kline is a native of Philadelphia, where he was born on the 19th of October 1824. While yet a boy he had a strong penchant for gathering anything odd or curious that tell in his way. Old coins and medals naturally attracted his attention and his well known cabinet was sold in June 1855.

Since that time he has been interested in quite a number of sales, some of them (in consequence, probably, of pecuniary troubles) under the name of his wife Mrs. A. C. Kline. He has, of course, in so long a connection with numismatics, brought to the surface some of the rarest pieces of this country, among which may be mentioned a "Naked bust Washington" and New Jersey "Carthago."

ʔ June 21 | M. W. Dickeson | T. Birch & Son | Phia. |
                             | p. | 1 | 16 | 476 | $

, This was also printed on one side only of each page.

, Sept. 5 | Mr. Elliot | G. A. Leavitt & Co. | N. Y. |
                             | p. & n. | 2 | 36 | 901 | $1059.00

Sept. 13 | M. W. Dickeson | T. Birch & Son | Phia. |
                             | p. | 1 | 15 | 493 | $

Sept. 28 | M. W. Dickeson | T. Birch & Son | Phia. |
                             | p. | 1 | 12 | 344 | $

Montroville W. Dickeson, M. D., the owner of the above collection as also of numerous others of a similar character, is a native of Philadelphia, where he was born June 18th, 1809.

He is a physician by education, but by nature an observer and a collector; eager in the pursuit of knowledge, whether in the hospital or school of the white man, or in the wigwam, or by the council-fire of the red.

Nothing comes amiss to him, mineral, shell, or flower, ammonites or birds eggs, stone axes, darics, or electrotypes, cowrie, wampum, or coin.

While thus energetic in seeking information, he is equally willing to impart to his fellow-man the results of his investigations: two qualities not frequently found combined in the same individual; a combination which makes a man truly useful to his fellow-man.

Prof. Dickeson is also the author of the well-known work, "The American Numismatic Manual," a work which has met with so much favor from numismatists, that it has passed a third edition, which is even now, "scarce."

Dr. Dickeson should carefully revise the work, should he issue another edition and correct some errors and omissions of which none know better than he.

Oct. 5 | John A. Nexsen | Bangs, Merwin & Co. | N. Y. |
                           | p. & n. | 2 | 39 | 868 | $1263.00

A "List of Prices" was issued by the N. E. Numismatic Archæological Society, susequent to the sale.

Oct. 12 | | T. Birch & Son | Phia. |
                           | p. | 1 | 1 | 326 | $

A broadside sheet catalogue of coins, medals, minerals, and curiosities.

Oct. 23 | J. Ledyard Hodge | W. L. Wall & Co. | Washington |
                           | p. | 1 | 1 | 57 | $335.25

In this little sheet (6x11), were offered 256 pieces, many of them proofs, all beings U. S. coins of silver, copper, and nickel.

Oct. 25 | M. W. Dickeson | T. Birch & Son | Phia. |
                           | p. | 1 | 1 | 322 | $

A broadside sheet, printed in three columns; it comprises coins, minerals, and curiosities.

Oct. 30 | | Bangs, Merwin & Co. | N. Y. |
                           | | 1 | 14 | 297 | $0.20

Lot 156 in this book-sale was described as follows :
        "13 Copper Coins, Republic Française and S. America."
sold for 1½ cents each.

Nov. 7 | | T. Birch & Son | Phia. |
                           | p. | 1 | 19 | 487 | $

๑ Nov. 13 | Edward Cogan | Bangs, Merwin & Co. | N. Y. |
               | p. & n. | 1 | 26 | 416 | $ 460.24

๑ Dec. 5 | Dr. Charles Clay | G. A. Leavitt & Co. | N. Y. |
               | p. & n. | 3 | 97 | 1356 | $6241.50

The same with 1 plate of photograph illustrations.
ᐩ The same with 2 plates of photograph illustrations.
Soon after the sale, a "List of prices" was issued by the N. E. Numismatic and Archæological Society, but proving to be incorrect, that Society, early in 1872, issued a corrected edition.
Messrs. W. E. Woodward and W. H. Strobridge also contributed slightly to the above sale.

Dec. 19 | Stanislaus Jansen | A. B. Miner & Bro. | N. Y. |
              | | 1 | 8 | 150 | $

This sale consisted principally of clothing and jewelry, there were some half dozen or more lots of coins and medals.

Dec. 21 | M. W. Dickeson | Thomas E. Kirby & Co. | Phia. |
              | | 1 | 19 | 501 | $

The following is described as lot,
"154.   Lava from Vesuvius in which there is a Silver Coin."

1872.

⌐ Jan. 5 | Brinley Robinson *et al.* | Bangs, Merwin & Co. | N.Y.|
               | p. & n. | 1 | 14 | 454 | $221.32

Jan. 20 | | A. B. Miner & Bro. | N. Y. |
              | | 1 | 15 | 238 | $

This catalogue exhibits a decidedly odd way of numerating lots. The first five lots being distinguished from each other by O's, one to five in number, then the letters of the alphabet in consecutive order, first singly, then doubled. Thus the first lot is described as lot :
              " O   91 pes rare and curious European Silver Coins."
              "OO   105 pes rare and curious European Silver Coins."

ᐨ Feb. 19 | J. K. Curtis | Bangs, Merwin & Co. | N. Y. |
               | p. & n. | 1 | 14 | 370 | $103.62

· April 8 | | T. Birch & Son | Phia. |
| p. & n. | 3 | 52 | 1456 | $1048.97

This was quite a good collection, comprising a general variety of ancient and modern coins. Catalogued by Mason & Co.

April 11 | Benj. Haines | G. A. Leavitt & Co. | N. Y. |
| p. & n. | 2 | 40 | 883 | $857.08

April 11 | Benj. Haines | G. A. Leavitt & Co.|N.Y.|
| Addenda | P. & N. | 1 | 1 | 10 | $7.65

This collection, besides coins, also comprised coin catalogues, paper-money, postage-stamps, etc. The addenda was sold from manuscript, of which 5 copies on note and 20 on plain paper, have been since privately printed.

May 7 | E. J. Cleveland | Bangs, Merwin & Co. | N. Y. |
| p. & n. | 2 | 72 | 1384 | $990.48

Addenda of one lot of coins sold to Mr. E. Cogan for $101.00.

Of the collection the latter portion in the catalogue were books. 1272 lots only were sold, the remainder of the books were withdrawn.

June 6 | E. King, Sr. | A. B. Miner & Bro. | N. Y. |
| | 1 | 16 | 255 | $

This collection consisted of 199 lots of coins, the remainder, books, etc. But few of the coins were sold; the prices offered being unsatisfactory to the owner.

Oct. 29 | C. N. Bodey | T. Birch & Son | Phia. |
| p. & n. | 2 | 29 | 600 | $935.36

The same printed on tinted paper.

Nov. 11 | Edward Cogan | Bangs, Merwin & Co. | N. Y. |
| p. & n. | 1 | 31 | 719 | $532.99

The same uncut.

Dec. 12 | Furman, Carnes *et al.* | G. A. Leavitt & Co. | N.Y. |
| p. & n. | 3 | 60 | 1103 | $1826.54

| Addenda bound in | | 1 | 2 | 25 | $

| Addenda No. 2 | Geo. A. Leavitt & Co. | N. Y. |
| p. & n. | 1 | 1 | 25 | $66.66

38 copies of the catalogue were issued with one plate of photograph-illustrations; a few copies were also issued, printed on one side of each page only, and interleaved. Subsequent to the sale, a list of prices was published by the N. E. Numismatic Society.

Dec. 18 | John W. Haseltine | T. Birch & Son | Phia. |
| p. & n. | 1 | 20 | 346 | $1174.83

The same printed on only one side of each page.
The same printed on large paper.

1873.

Jan. 28 | C. A. Leveridge | Bangs, Merwin & Co. | N. Y. |
| p. & n. | 1 | 27 | 638 | $402.52

| Addenda | Bangs, Merwin & Co. | N. Y. |
| P. & N. | 1 | 1 | 3 | $0.95

Of this collection it is needless to say much, and of the prices for which the pieces sold still less; had it not been for the intrinsic value of a number of the pieces, the general average would not have been maintained.

The pieces described in the addenda were sold from manuscript, 20 copies of which have since been privately printed.

Jan. 30 | Dr. R. V. Aulick | Lattimer & Cleary | Washington |
| p. & n. | 2 | 12 | 305 | $

I have not yet seen a copy of this catalogue either fully named or priced.

Feb. 5 | T. P. Rossiter | Messrs. Leavitt | N. Y. |
| p. & n. | 4 | 39 | 693 | $14.50

10 copies of the catalogue were printed on heavy paper, interleaved. This collection belonged to the well-known artist, through whose decease it came before the public. It was the collection of an artist, not of a numismatist, for there were but four coins (which sold for $14.50) in the entire collection, which consisted chiefly of paintings, antiques, costumes, and other paraphernalia of a painter and brought nearly $13,000.

Feb. 11 | | T. Birch & Son | Phia. |
| p. & n. | 1 | 13 | 349 | $112.00

About half of this collection consisted of ancient roman and greek coins.

〇 Feb. 25 | S. W. Chubbuck | T. Birch & Son | Phia. |
         | p. & n. | 4 | 127 | 2896 | $2927.44

The same illustrated with five plates of photographs.
The same illustrated as the last, but printed on only one side of each page.
The same as the last, but without the illustrations.

March 12 | John W. Kline | Bangs, Merwin & Co. | N. Y. |
         | p. & n. | 1 | 29 | 616 | $202.38

   ⌒ | F. M. Bird, | Bangs, Merwin & Co. | N.Y. |
      Addenda | p. & n. | 1 | 2 | 36 | $20.65

April 9 | Alexander Balmanno | T. Birch & Son | Phia. |
         | p. & n. | 1 | 24 | 572 | $468.53

4 copies of the above were printed on large tinted paper.
This catalogue was also issued printed on only one side of each leaf.
Mr. Balmanno's only reason for parting with his nucleus of a fine collection, could probably only have been to "let go and take a better hold," for he has since then taken a greater interest and has succeeded in obtaining some of the finest numismatic gems and rarities of ancient and modern times. Not this alone, but he is peering into prehistoric times, seeking knowledge in the bronzes and stone implements of the "long ago."

April 16 | Mrs. De H. Hazard | Robert Somerville | N. Y. |
         | | 1 | 16 | 228 | $

· On page 8, lot 102½ of this catalogue is described as follows :
"Old Coins and Pencil, found in Cæsar's Palace."

〇 May 15 | E. McK. Holley | Messrs. Leavitt | N. Y. |
         | p. & n. | 3 | 74 | 1036 | $49.46

Same illustrated with a photograph plate of engraved gems.
This collection contained but few coins; (which, sold for $49.46,) was extremely rich in works of art, whether paintings, bronzes, carved precious stones, arms or armor, and afforded a delightful opportunity to compare the past with the present. The entire collection brought nearly $5000.

May 19 | Isaac F. Wood | Bangs, Merwin & Co. | N. Y. |
         | p. & n. | 3 | 107 | 1853 | $3516.94

Same, uncut.
This collection was one exceedingly interesting to American collectors, whether on this side of the great lakes or the other. The owner was the well-known and diligent librarian of the American Numismatic and Archæological Society, who, though parting with his coins, still held fast to his "Numismatic Library," which is probably one of the richest "this side of the water."

June 9 | Edward Cogan | Bangs, Merwin & Co. | N. Y. |
| p. & n. | 3 | 73 | 1365 | $1647.25

√ Same, uncut.

In this collection Mr. Cogan offered a good variety, with quite a number of fine pieces.

June 18 | | Leonard & Co. | Boston |
| | 1 | 19 | 488 | $

A book sale, but lot 414 is described as,

"A variety of Coins very old, Silver and Copper; Minerals, Shells, Curiosities, etc."

June 18 | Loring G. Parmelee | Messrs. Leavitt | N. Y. |
| p. & n. | 3 | 76 | 1202 | $2272.01

This collection comprised duplicates. Mr. Parmelee having purchased Mr. Seavey's cabinet, and chosen therefrom such additions, as he desired, placed the remainder before the public for competition. It, of course, contained many fine and rare pieces.

Mr. Loring G. Parmelee was born in the town of Wilmington, Vt., May 7th, 1827; he removed to Boston in 1849, where he established himself as a baker, which vocation he still pursues. His business naturally threw in his way many copper coins, observing the oddity of many of these, he commenced placing aside the early colonial pieces and the regular issues of the mint; as fortune favored him, he replaced poor by better specimens, occasionally making slight purchases, as he became more familiar with the rarity and value of pieces; in 1865 he made a single purchase to the amount of $200 from Mr. Ahlborn, the well-known Boston dealer. Thus far Mr. Parmelee had confined himself almost exclusively to the copper coinage of which he had now a fine collection. His purchase of the Seavey collection, at once placed him among the leaders in numismatic collections, he has since purchased the American portion of the Adams, and lately the entire collection of Mr. J. Carson Brevoort. The purchase of these cabinets, in addition to the purchases of several smaller collections, has undoubtedly placed his cabinet at the head of all collectors in this country, in his specialties, the colonial and mint series of coins, whether of gold, silver, or copper. In disposing of the above collection it must be borne in mind that Mr. Parmelee disposed only of duplicates, as was also the case with his sale of June 1876, excepting of course all coins or medals, which are not included in his special lines.

June 26 | | T. Birch & Son | Phia. |
| p. & n. | 1 | 8 | 148 | $153.96

Sept. 22 | C. A. Leveridge | Bangs, Merwin & Co. | N. Y. |
| p. & n. | 2 | 39 | 1512 | $424.96

Oh, dear! of "Coins which a few months ago had small value," it is to be feared that this sale gave them a smaller one.

$\mathcal{O}$ Sept. 24 | J. McAllister | Messrs. Leavitt | N. Y. |
| p. & n. | 4 | 96 | 1625 | $1726.49

' Same, with one plate of photograph illustrations.
' Same, with two pages of photograph illustrations.
Same, 5 copies with illustrations, and interleaved with red tissue paper.

Sept. 24 | Addenda | Messrs. Leavitt | N. Y. |
| P. P. | 1 | 1 | 4 | $1.55

This collection belonged to the above-named gentleman, more familiarly known to the American people as the "Wizard of the North" from his feats of presti-digitation, with which but few, probably, are not familiar. He seems to have found some time to devote to a higher pursuit when not practising the "Black Art." Let us hope that the sale of his collection did not mean a permanent withdrawal from numismatics, but that in his travels, he will seek and find other gems, with which to return among us.

The addenda was sold from manuscript, 20 copies of which have been since privately printed. The collection of catalogues was the property of Mr. Geo. B. Mason.

$\mathcal{O}$ Oct. 13 | F. H. Schultze | Bangs, Merwin & Co. | N. Y. |
| p. & n. | 2 | 35 | 920 | $408.23

This small sized catalogue was issued with a title page, which ignored the auctioneers and days of sale, all of which had to be written in. The collection consisted principally of coins of the German States, which, however interesting in Europe, are as yet not much appreciated in this country, and many of the pieces were sold for less than their value as bullion. An additional lot, a coin-cabinet was sold for $5.75.

' Nov. 6 | C. A. Leveridge | Bangs, Merwin & Co. | N. Y. |
| p. & n. | 2 | 37 | 976 | $181.75

Mr. "GOINTOEM STRONG," who, a number of years ago, offered an *extremely curious, rare, and unique collection* at public sale, but, at the last moment, withdrew it entirely, possibly with a feeling of contempt for his unappreciative audience, must have rejoiced at the wisdom he displayed at that time in acting as he did, thus avoid-ing the "slaughter" which befell his more rash successor. What must have been his "phelings" to see lot 15 sold for "Five Cents;" lot 53 for "Three Cents;" lot 126 for "25 Cents;" lot 165 for "eight cents," and similiar prices for other equally rare pieces, and some, heretofore, unknown coins and medals. We are left in ignorance of the name of the gentleman, to whom Mr. Lilliendahl sold the catalogue to, or what price he obtained for it, (*vide* 859.) It would afford the writer much pleasure to see the catalogue alluded to in lot 867. Lot 883 "puzzles me intirely," as *Pat* would say.

Nov. 10 | Patterson | Messrs. Leavitt | N. Y. |
                                      | | 1 | 11 | 174 | $1.60

In this catalogue is the following described lot :
"149 Set of Scientific Medals, (in Case)." 16 pieces sold at 10 cts. each.

Nov. 20 | Edward Cogan | Bangs, Merwin & Co. | N. Y. |
                               | p. & n. | 2 | 42 | 847 | $1088.79

Some fine rare pieces were in this collection.

Nov. 24 | E. McK. Holley | Messrs. Leavitt | N. Y. |
                               | p. & n. | 3 | 32 | 464 | $12.00

Antiques, Bronzes, Gems, etc. The following two lots might mislead into the
idea that they were medals, which they were not.
"318 Electrotype in Oak Frame, Surrender of Lord Conwallis."
"319 Electrotype in Oak Frame, Columbus."

1874.

⓪ Jan. 13 | J. W. Haseltine | T. Birch & Son | Phia. |
                               | p. & n. | 3 | 48 | 1106 | $1630.52

⑧ Feb. 11 | C. A. Leveridge | Bangs, Merwin & Co. | N. Y. |
                               | p. & n. | 2 | 32 | 845 | $226.50

⓪ Feb. 17 | John Campbell | T. Birch & Son | Phia. |
                               | p. & n. | 3 | 39 | 1139 | $983.05

⑦ Feb. 23 | W. E. Woodward | Messrs. Leavitt | N. Y. |
                               | p. & n. | 4 | 85 | 1852 | $2680.12

Same uncut.
Mr. Woodward presented this catalogue, prepared by Mr. Strobridge, as his
"18th sale." Though not quite up in the quality or rarity of the pieces offered in
many of his collections, yet it will well pay to review. A few pieces belonged to
another party.

Ⓒ March 18 | E. McK. Holley | Messrs. Leavitt | N. Y. |
                               | p. & n. | 4 | 60 | 1158 | $29.70

Same uncut.
Another of this gentleman's valuable collections of antiques, accompanied by a few
coins.
The total proceeds were nearly $5000.

April 7 | Daniel E. Groux | Messrs. Leavitt | N. Y. |
          | p. & n. | 3 | 57 | 1173 | $1452.76

, The same, illustrated with a photographic plate.
This was probably the last portion of the collection of the noted Frenchman, who commenced some twenty-five years ago to hold forth his collection as one of almost fabulous value. Great in number it undoubtedly was, some pieces were certainly rare, but all were by him over-estimated. His undoubted industry in seeking and tracing out the origin and *"raison d'être"* was with him a labor of love, with a hope at the same time, that it would prove remunerative. The following, which was a marginal note by his own hand, copied from one of the volumes, (Second Vol., No. 25, June 21, 1730) of his numismatic library, will best serve to show the straits in which he, at times, found himself—"home! D. E. Groux 3 March 1857 Boston No. 1 Lagrange Place — have finished to-day to translate Extracts of these 7 Vol. [KOHLER's MUNZ BELUSTIGUNG] and other works in French Spanish Danish and poor me after the finishing of my herculean work I have hardly bread and all my poor things are pledged, Griddy America is a poor land for Scientific men D. E. Groux." It was undoubtedly in one of these straits that he, an enthusiast himself, sufficiently inspired a lady of his acquaintance, a resident of Washington, with a sufficient *enthusiasm*, to induce her to loan him several times its value, upon the collection which he placed in her hands as security for the loan. Years rolled on, loan nor interest being paid, till death removed the numismatist from his earthly idols, which, after a further lapse of years, were at this time brought under the hammer.

May 5 | James Parker *et al.* | Bangs, Merwin & Co. | N. Y. |
          | p. & n. | 4 | 94 | 2073 | $4204.15

This was a large and fine collection, comprising coins and medals of the leading nations, as well as a small variety of Continental paper money. Mr. James Parker was born in Hollis, New Hampshire, in 1816. For a greater portion of his life he was engaged on railroads; in latter years he took an active part in politics, being twice elected to Congress. He was of a genial, affable disposition, a sincere and devoted student in the science of numismatology for many years. He died in January 1874, regretted by all of his wide circle of friends and acquaintances.

June 9 | Benjamin Haines | Messrs. Leavitt | N. Y. |
          | p. & n. | 3 | 26 | 874 | $621.25

A small collection of almost everything in the way of curiosities.

June 17 | Francis T. Hagadorn | T. Birch & Son | Phia. |
          | p. & n. | 1 | 15 | 287 | $272.36

A small collection of coins, autographs and curiosities.

June 18 | E. McK. Holley | Messrs. Leavitt | N. Y. |
          | p. & n. | 5 | 73 | 1429 | $3800.01

This collection, which contained a few medals, consisted chiefly of antique and rare pottery, bronzes, armor, and bric-a-brac.

○ Sept. 24 | Edward Cogan | Bangs, Merwin & Co. | N. Y. |
                             | p. & n. | 1 | 22 | 527 | $696.52

   ○ | Mr. Markgrass | Bangs, Merwin & Co. | N. Y. |
               | Addenda | p. & n. | 1 | 3 | 80 | $125.81

The addenda which is bound in, forming part of the catalogue, belonged, as
stated, to Mr. Markgrass.

○ Oct. 6 | Edward Middleton | Messrs. Leavitt | N. Y. |
                             | p. & n. | 4 | 95 | 1272 | $2399.29

      | Addenda bound in | Messrs. Leavitt | N. Y. |
                       | p. & n. | 1 | 11 | 480 | $

   ○ Same uncut.
   ○ Same with two illustrations (photographic).
A few copies of the above catalogue (without covers), terminating at lot 1210,
were privately issued a few months previous.
This cabinet of ancient coins, the property of Commodore Middleton, was
without a rival in the United States, in the beauty and number of its gems. In
either branch, Imperial, Family, or Colonial, it stood pre-eminent and well
worthy the able efforts of Mr. W. H. Strobridge, who catalogued the collection,
who found himself at home in this his favorite branch of numismatology. But
neither his extensive researches, able descriptions, nor the undenied merits of the
collection, could prevent the anticipated result of a heavy sacrifice and loss on the
part of the owner.   Americans are not yet (distasteful as the confession may be),
equal in education or appreciation to the absorption, at a fair value, of so large a
collection of ancient coins.   Yet, the patriotic Commodore chose rather to con-
tribute heavily to the education of his fellow-countrymen, than to send his collection to Europe to be sold, as advised by some to do.   The seed thus sown has not
been unproductive of good, for at some subsequent sales, prices have been paid
which, though not quite equal to their value in Europe, nevertheless show a marked
advance, and a tacit sign of advancement in the appreciation of the merits of
ancient art, as displayed on their coins and medals.

○ Nov. 27 | C. Harrison Sandford | Bangs, Merwin & Co.|N. Y.|
                             | p. & n. | 1 | 20 | 367 | $2871.80
   ' Same uncut.
   ○ ' Same with two plates of photographic illustrations.
That so small a collection should bring so high a sum, is the best evidence of
the quality of the pieces it contained.   Almost exclusively American in character,
it is in striking contrast with the collection last mentioned.   The oldest and the
youngest nations are thus closely in contact.

Dec. 1 | | Thomas & Sons | Phia. |
                       | | 1 | 1 | 255 | $
On this broadside sheet is lot
          "133   567   Coins and Medals."

Dec. 1 | A. M. Cristalar | R. Somerville | N. Y. |
     | | | 40 | 753 | $

Same, 6 copies interleaved.

This was the entire collection contained in the well-known "Old Curiosity Shop" on Broadway, even a close examination of the catalogue gives little idea of the rare and curious articles of *virtù* which were "knocked down" by the auctioneer, under direction of the Sheriff; it was indeed a "slaughter." The following is a fair exhibit of the clearness and distinctness with which many of the articles were catalogued. Lot,

"675   box old Coin."

In those ten letters were comprised hundreds of coins and medals, good, bad, and indifferent, rare and common. "SIC TRANSIT." The *transit* from the glowing descriptions of Messrs. Strobridge or Cogan, to such descriptions is enough to make antiquarians *sic*.

Dec. 14 | | Bangs, Merwin & Co. | N. Y. |
     | p. & n. | 1 | 8 | 166 | $31.48

Amidst engravings and curiosities are some 18 different lots of medals on pages 6 and 8, which sold for the sum stated, $31.48.

Dec. 14 | Charles D. Lathrop *et al.* | Messrs. Leavitt | N. Y. |
     | | | 59 | 1079 |

The sale of this collection was postponed to the 21st.

Dec. 16 | Edward Cogan | Bangs, Merwin & Co. | N. Y. |
     | p. & n. | 2 | 48 | 875 | $468.40

Dec. 21 | Charles D. Lathrop *et al.* | Messrs. Leavitt | N. Y. |
     | p. & n. | 3 | 59 | 1079 | $1947.69

Same, published on tinted paper.

Dec. 22 | Charles Wild | Messrs. Leavitt | N. Y. |
     | Addenda | p. & n. | 1 | 1 | 32 | $50.32

This collection was formed from the cabinets of Messrs. J. Hobart Smith, F. I. Ilsley, Charles D. Lathrop, E. Loder, and E. J. Attinelli. Mr. Charles Wild contributing the greater portion of the addenda. Mr. Smith's portion will be found in the rare and beautiful ancient coins.

1875.

9 Jan. 25 | Henry Ahlborn *et al.* | Messrs. Leavitt | N. Y. |
                    | p. & n. | 4 | 78 | 2022 | $1571.20

The greater portion of this collection belonged to a widow lady of Cambridge, whose modesty and timidity prevent the publication of her name.

Mr. Henry Ahlborn, who was a part owner of the above collection, is the well known dealer who is located at the "Old Toll House," foot of Cambridge Street, Boston.

Mr. Ahlborn is a native of Hanover, Germany, where he was born April 17th, 1835, he immigrated to this country in 1855, settling at Dedham, Mass., where he worked at his trade, being a tailor. In 1860 he removed to Boston, where he settled himself at the Old Toll House, which is still his present location; there he commenced putting aside such of the old cents as came in his way; showing these to friends, he began exchanging and selling to improve his own little collection. Having extravagantly spent at one time five dollars for coins, in a purchase from Mr. Chadbourne, a domestic cloud arose, which soon passed away, on his disposing of said coins at a profit. This little transaction led to others, which also proving profitable, the sky remained serene; thus he became a dealer, and now Mr. Ahlborn remains undisturbed, no matter to what extent he may purchase his "old coins." This reminds me of a friend's position in a neighboring city, who has decided hobbies not merely in old coins, but other antiquities; immediately on his appearing at home "with another package of that old trash," and similar good-natured remarks, to which our friend silently and quietly submits, until next day, when he makes another appearance with another package, termed, "a sop to Cerberus," in the shape of a new bonnet or a dress, which at once so fully engages the attention of his "better half," that he can safely open his package, and feast his eyes upon a *genuine* finely patinated medallion of, well say, the Emperor OTHO, or a less rare but more antique stone battle-axe, or jug of some pre-Adamite ancestor of Inca the First.

1 March 1 | Edward Cogan | Bangs, Merwin & Co. | N. Y. |
                    | p. & n. | 2 | 38 | 818 | $1188.40

0 April 13 | | T. Birch & Son | N. Y. |
                    | p. & n. | 2 | 33 | 781 | $1215.02

" April 28 | Joseph E. Gay *et al.* | Messrs. Leavitt | N. Y. |
                    | p. & n. | 4 | 100 | 1809 | $2813.75

ʎ Same issued on tinted paper.

A portion of the same, comprising that part belonging to Mr. J. E. Gay, was issued printed on fine paper. 47 pp., 704 lots, principally British and Ancient coins.

May 7 | Edward Cogan | Bangs, Merwin & Co. | N. Y. |
                    | p. & n. | 1 | 27 | 517 | $807.59

_ϕ_ May 17 | George Stenz | Messrs. Leavitt | N. Y.
| p. & n. | 6 | 236 | 3871 | $6547.96

This collection, which consisted principally of coins and medals of the various German Principalities, was probably the largest collection ever offered in this country, in point of number of pieces, many of them in extremely fine condition, and well worthy the great labor and research bestowed in the preparation of the catalogue by Mr. W. H. Strobridge. While it is to be regretted that the pecuniary result to the owner must have produced a loss, yet the catalogue on which so much care and labor was bestowed, must ever remain a work of the greatest instruction and utility to the American collector seeking information relative to the branch of coins principally treated upon. It is true, that there are many learned works which go over the ground more fully perhaps, yet they are almost exclusively written in the Latin or German languages. This catalogue may be indeed termed a "Pocket Epitome of Teutonic Coins."

June 26 | A. Cristalar | J. Johnson | N. Y. |
| | 1 | 14 | 167 | $

This sale comprised furniture, bric-a-brac, etc.; on pp. 11 and 12 are described seven lots of gold, silver, and copper coins.

_ϕ_ June 30 | Edward Cogan | Bangs, Merwin & Co. | N. Y. |
| p. & n. | 1. | 27 | 694 | $490.55

July 12 | | T. Birch & Son | Phia. |
| p. & n. | 1 | 23 | 504 | $516.29

_ν_ Oct. 7 | J. W. Haseltine | T. Birch & Son | Phia. |
| | 1 | 24 | 500 | $219.07

_ϕ_ Oct. 25 | M. J. Cohen | Bangs, Merwin & Co. | N. Y. |
| p. & n. | 5 | 102 | 2400 | $9744.03

What the Stenz collection was to German coins, this collection is to American mint issues in particular, few of which were missing. Colonial pieces were also well represented, as were also the British Series; several of the rarest of which were to be found in this celebrated collection. Of the rarity and beauty of many of the American pieces it is needless to speak, as the catalogue itself (the work of Mr. Cogan) shows faithfully enough. Fine and rich though the collection was, its sale was not a success, which could only be attributed to the unfortunate enforced absence, through sickness, of Mr. Edward Cogan, under whose supervision the sale was to have taken place; that absence was severely felt by all, and probably by no one more than Mr. Cohen.

Nov. 16 | J. H. Taylor & H. Ahlborn | Messrs. Leavitt | N. Y. |
| p. & n. | 5 | 123 | 2389 | $4552.53

This large and fine collection, consisting chiefly of American coins, was in a greater part the property of the late James H. Taylor, the well-known numismatist of Charleston, S. C., whose decease placed this subject of his earnest attention before the public for competition and dispersion. His contributions to numismatology through the columns of the Numismatic Journal, rendered his name familiar to collectors, who were eagerly on hand to secure some coveted prize. Mr. Henry Ahlborn is the well-known dealer at the "Old Toll House", foot of Cambridge St., Boston.

○ Dec. 6 | J. W. Haseltine | T. Birch & Son | Phia. |
          | p. & n. | 4 | 76 | 1952 | $1837.24

Dec. 15 | | Field, Morris, Fenner & Co. | N. Y. |
         | | 1 | 36 | 629 |

Lots 531 @ 542 inclusive are :
          "Tortoise Shell Cigar Cases inlaid with Japanese Coin."
Lots 583 @ 591 are gold and silver Japanese coins.

Dec. 17 | Hall &   Maxwell | Messrs. Leavitt | N. Y. |
         | p. | 5 | 67 | 1097 | .$43.86

| Addenda | Messrs. Leavitt | N. Y. |
            . | p. | 1 | 10 | 231 | $

This was a collection principally of Ceramic ware, it also included many objects of art in wood, metal, etc. On pages 65 and 66 are several lots of coins and medals. Another of Mr. Strobridge's interesting catalogues. A few copies were also issued on fine paper.

◌ Dec. 22 | John W. Haseltine | Thomas Birch & Son | Phia. |
          | | 1 | 16 | 369 | $1.00

The following is described as Lot :
          "233   Old Spanish Dollar from a wrecked ship"

PART II

CATALOGUES AND PRICE-LISTS

Issued by Institutions, Dealers, or Private Individuals.

1764.

The Charter Laws and Catalogue of the Books of the Library Company of Philadelphia.

" Communiter bona profundere Deum est."
Philadelphia:
Printed by B. Franklin and D. Hall.
M,DCC,LXIV.

On pages 145 to 148 of the above-entitled Catalogue the following mention is made :

" The valuable Collection of ancient MEDALS, in the Library, was received from ENGLAND *(through the hands of the Honorable Proprietary,* THOMAS PENN, *Esq.,) with the following Remarks and Account of them :*

The *Roman* coins hereafter mentioned are a small Specimen of the several Sorts of Money made Use of in that famous Empire, and are a Present from Mr. GRAY, of *Colchester,* to the public Library at Philadelphia, as a Token of the Honor and Esteem which he has for that Colony,

Medals, merely considered as Curiosities, are of very little Value, and hardly worth the Attention of prudent Men; but when they are regarded as Proofs and Illustrations of History, or when the Legends or Reverses contain any useful Instruction, some Benefit may be obtained from them.

The two first of the Silver are Consular, and struck before the Time of the Emperors. That with the head of CERES, and the Oxen at Plow on the Reverse, may not only allude to the superstitious Ceremony used upon marking out a new Colony, but to the Agriculture upon which the public Welfare depends. The other, with the Horseman on the Reverse, regards purely the military Glory of which that People were so fond, and which at last proved their Ruin, when their old Laws were turned into a military Government.

The first of the two is the properest Present to PENNSYLVANIA, though something may be learned from the latter: A military Force, for necessary Self-defence, is often wanted, to preserve what Industry has gained ; but it never should be allowed to extend itself so far as to endanger what it is designed to protect.

Though we ought not to let our Trust in Providence run into Presumption, or to the Neglect of those Means which are put into our Hands; yet there is something more to be expected of Security to this Province than to any other, because they set out upon a better Foundation. There is hardly an Instance in the World, of a People's growing to such a Number, and such a Degree of Strength, without any one War or military Enterprize.

It is most ardently to be wished, that the same Virtue with which they began, and have hitherto continued, may remain as their Support for Ages to come. While their Virtue, their Liberty, and their Moderation last, their Security will, in all Probability, continue.

The Silver Imperial Medals, any of the Books upon that Subject will explain, and for want of Time they are but very slightly mentioned in the Catalogue.

As to the first of the Silver, it may be observed that the Workmanship of it is GREEK, and far superior to any that follow.

The *Grecian* Free States, (which some of our Northern Colonies resemble), carried all Arts and Sciences into the greatest Perfection.

The Medaillion of *Vespasian* is quite a Picture of him, as are also most of the rest; but, as the Empire declined, the Work grew worse. At best, it did not come up to the *Greek*.

The Palladium on the Reverse of *Vespasian's* Coin, and many others, was probably emblematical. It was a Gift of *Minerva*, that is *Wisdom;* and while that was with them, *Rome* was safe.

The last in the card of *M. Aurelius* is of very good work.

That of *Magnentius*, in middle Brass, with the Christian Ensign upon it, is very barbarous and mean. The gross Barbarism of those Times on the one Hand, and the *Platonic* Refinements on the other, were enough to destroy any Thing but absolute Truth.

The Medals in small Brass, of *Constantine* and the rest, are good and well preserved, and that of *Helena* not easily to be met with. She was our Townswoman, and we have several authentic Memorials of her.

The last, of *Rome,* with the Wolf on the Reverse, and the Founders of the City sucking her, is emblematical likewise, and to be found on many of the Medals of the higher Empire. If the *Romans* would, by this, have been put in Mind of their Original, and preserved their Humility, a Virtue they often practised in their best Times (though they never pretended to it, nor had even a Name for it as a Virtue) it would have saved their State, and stopped the Luxury which proved their Ruin.

A R G E N T I.

1. *Caput Cereris.* CAECIAN. *L. Cassius. a. Cæcio adoptatus.* L. CASSIUS. *Boves jugati.* Coloniam vel agrorum *divisionem respicientes ;* v. Vaillant, 244.

2. ROMA. *Caput Urbi.* Q. M. SERGI. SILVS, *Figura equestris, caput et gladium sinistra tenens, in memoriam M. Sergij Sili, fortitudine clarissimi, qui dextra perdita, sinistra sæpius pugnavit ;* v. ib., 395.

3. TRAIANO, &c. *Roma sedens dextra Palladium tenet.*

4. TRAIANO, &c. S. P. Q. R. *Senatus Populusque Romanus,* OPTIMO PRINCIPI. *Figura sacrificans.*

5. TRAIAN, *Victoria alata* COS IIII.

6. HADRIANVS, *Mars gradiens.*

7. ANTONINVS PIVS.

8. DIVVS ANTONINVS CONSECRATIO. *Rogus,*

9. FAVSTINA. *Antonini.* PIETAS AVG,

10. FAVSTINA. *M. Aurelii.*
11. IVLIA AVGVSTA. *Severi Uxor.*
12. ALEXANDER SEV.
13. IVLIANVS *Apostata.* VOTIS.

ÆRIS *Numisma maximum Medallion, primi Moduli.*

1. IMP. CAES. VESPASIAN. AVG. P. M. T. R. P. ROMA. *Stans, hastam purare sinistra tenens, dextra Palladium.*
2. IMP. CAES. NERVAE TRAIANO GER. DAC. S. P. Q. R. OPTIMO PRINCI-PI. *Roma sedens.*
3. ANTONINVS AVG. PIVS. *Figura sacrificans.*
4. DIVA FAVSTINA. *Figura stans dextra globa tenet.*
5. ANTONINVS PIVS. *Figura stans læva cornucopiam.*
6. ANT. PIVS. *Figura dextra globum.*
7. M. ANTONINVS AUG. FIDES EXERCITVVM. *Miles Romanus signum militam sinistra tenens.*
8. *Idem M. Aurelius.* T. R. POT. &c.
9. IMP. GORDIANVS, &c. AETERNITATI AVG.
10. GORDIANVS. *Pacis vel tranquilitatis publicos symbolum sedens.*
11. GORDIANVS.
12. GORDIANVS. *Virtutis Symbolum.*
13. ALEXANDER SEVERVS.
14. PHILLIPPVS.

ÆRIS. *Secundi Moduli.*

15. ANTONIA *Augusta.* *Caput Antoniæ.* TI. CLAVDIVS CAESAR. *Figura sacerdo-tis velata stans dextra simpulem gerens.*
16. DOMITIAN. *Fortuna.*
17. TRAIANVS. *Felicitas.*
18. FAVSTINA AVG. *Pii Aug. Filia. M. Aurelii Uxor.*
19. MAGVENTIVS. *Christi Monogramma.*
20. TRAIANVS *primæ formæ, Neptuni figura.*

ÆRIS. *Minimi Moduli.*

21 ad 29. CONSTANTINVS MAGNVS, *Helena* &c.

1770.

Catalogue of the Library Company of Philadelphia., 8vo., 350 pp.

On page 5 et seq., is described the before-mentioned collection.

1807.

A CATALOGUE of the Books belonging to the Library Company
of Philadelphia, to which is prefixed a short account of the
Institution, with the Charter, Laws, and Regulations.
" *Communiter Bona Profundere Decorum est.*"
Philadelphia. Printed by Bartran and Reynolds,
No. 58 North Second Street.
1807.

— Catalogue of the Library Company of Philadelphia.   8vo., 616 pp.

The title " Catalogue of Medals and Coins" is printed on page 589.   Then from
page 591 to page 600 both inclusive, is given a descriptive list of 379 Medals and
Coins of different countries, which formed the Cabinet of the Association at that
period.

1820.

CHARTER AND BYLAWS of the Athenæum of Philadelphia.   8vo.,
Philadelphia, 1820.

Contains a list of Coins and Medals.

1821.

" The East India Marine Society of Salem."   " W. Palfrey,
pr., 1821."   100 pp. 8vo.   Salem.

1822.

JAMES EASTBURN.   " A Catalogue of Books, including two
private libraries, and embracing an extensive collection of
very rare and valuable works in ancient and modern Literature, now on sale for cash, At the Literary Rooms, Broadway,
cor. of Pine street, New York, at the prices affixed.   by
JAMES EASTBURN.

Beneath a wood-cut in which, surrounded by books, is represented a figure of
Literature personified, who is repelling the advances of Father Time, is the following legend :

" *Multa renascentur, quæ jam cecidere, cadentque, quæ nunc sunt in
honore.*"

NEW YORK :

Printed by ABRAHAM PAUL, and to be had of J. EAST-
BURN, and of the principal Booksellers in the United States.
May, 1822.   (214 pp. 8vo.)

In the catalogue of which the above is a transcript of the title page, *verbatim et literatim*, on page 10, under the head of "*PORTRAITS AND PRINTS*," are described the following lots :

  91 Two Sets Medallions, $2.
  92 Two do.   do. $2.50.
  93 One do.   do. $3.

This catalogue has by some been classed among *Coin Catalogues*, though I must confess to the belief that it stands upon rather slender, if not untenable ground.

Mr. Eastman was a bookseller and kept a Reading Room at the place previously mentioned, he subsequently removed to Wall Street, residing at the time of his death, which took place the latter end of 1829 or early in 1830, at No. 89 Walker St.

1825.

REPORT of the SECOND ANNUAL Exhibition of the FRANK-LIN INSTITUTE of the State of PENNSYLVANIA, for the promotion of the Mechanic Arts.

Philadelphia.   Printed for the Institute, 1825.   (8vo. 52 pp.)

On pages 46 and 47 are the following descriptions of lots :

"393   Forty Medals struck at the United States' Mint, in Philadelphia, deposited by Adam Eckfeldt."

"543   An impression on Gypsum, of one of the dies now making by Christian Gobrecht for the Franklin Institute.

This die (which is the most important of the two required for the medal,) is finished, and it is hoped that the reverse die will be ready in a short time, so that the medals, awarded at this and the preceding Exhibition, may be soon distributed.—In justice to Mr. Gobrecht, the committee deem it proper to state, that many competent Judges have declared that this would prove one of the finest specimens of Die Sinking ever executed in the United States."

"637   A Medal of John Quincy Adams, President of the United States, executed at the United States' Mint in Philadelphia and deposited by Adam Eckfeldt."

1831.

The EAST INDIA MARINE SOCIETY of SALEM.
Salem Press.   Palfrey, Ives, Foote & Brown.
Date of Introduction Salem Oct. 1831.   178 pp.   8vo.   Salem.

1837.

"Supplement to the Catalogue of the articles in the Museum, Journals, &c. of the EAST INDIA MARINE SOCIETY of SALEM. Salem. Printed for the Society by William Ives & Co. 1837. 24 pp. 8vo.   Salem.

1839.

NATHAN DUNN'S, "Descriptive Catalogue of the Chinese Collection in Philadelphia. Written by E. C. Wines."
8vo. 103 pages.
Mentions on p. 48 some "Chinese Cash."

This collection was afterwards taken to London.

NATHAN DUNN'S "Descriptive Catalogue of the Chinese Collection in Philadelphia. (2d Edition 8vo. 120 pages.)

Lot 594 on Page 59 is described as follows :

"Ancient Chinese coins of different reigns. The inscriptions on them are in the antique seal character, which is a species of black letter in China. There are few persons who are well versed in it."

1840.

CATALOGUE of Books, Manuscripts, Maps, &c., added to the Library of the New York Historical Society since January 1839. (8vo. 32 pp.)   New York. 1840.

On page 29 are described an Elizabeth Shilling and a New Haven Medal of 1838.

1842.

CHINESE Museum Catalogue. 89 pp. 8vo.   New York.

CHINESE Museum Catalogue. 152 pp. 8vo.   Boston.
by John R. Peters Jr.

An article on coins on page 87.

" IMPORTANT Notice to all Colleges, State, and other Public Libraries," etc.   8 p. 8vo   New York.   1842.

In this pamphlet Mr. Ithiel Town offers to dispose of at private sale, " Books, Paintings, four or five hundred Coins, Medals, &c., in gold, silver, and copper."

1846.

CATALOGUE of the New York State Library.   294 pp.   8vo.
                                                              Albany.

On p. 290 is a descriptive list of medals, 8 in number.

1847.

CATALOGUE of the Chinese Museum.   Philadelphia.
   by John R. Peters Jr.

On pp. 95, 96, and 155 are articles, relating to coins.

1849.

CATALOGUE of the American Art Union.   New York.

On page 4 is a statement, relative to a distribution of Medals.

THOMPSON J.   Coin Chart Manual (No. 4)
   contains 750 illustrations of coins.   46 pp.   New York.

In connection with this Manual it may be proper here to say, that it was also issued with the imprint of other bankers and brokers.   The title pages being changed.   The illustrations being the same.

CATALOGUE of the Chinese Museum, by John R. Peters Jr.
   196 pp. 8vo.   New York.

Coins on pp. 101 and 152.

CATALOGUE of the Miscellaneous Books in the New York State Library.   8vo.   Albany.   1850.

Descriptive List of Medals on pp. 947 et seq.

1851.

DESCRIPTIVE CATALOGUE of Coins, Greek and Roman Medals belonging to the Historical Society of Maryland by D. E. Groux.

1852.

CATALOGUE of the Mercantile Library. First Supplement. N.Y.
Under the head of Miscellaneous on p. 35, some medals are described.

CATALOGUE of the State Cabinet of Natural History.   Albany.
On p. 88 is an interesting article on Silver Currency among the Indians.

1853.

CATALOGUE of Barnum's Museum.   112 pp.   New York.

CATALOGUE of the State Cabinet of Natural History.   Albany.

CATALOGUE of the Free Academy.   New York.
Has an illustration of the Ward Medal, and on page 33 a description of Medals.

OFFICIAL CATALOGUE of the Crystal Palace. 192 pp. New York.

The same.   "First Revised Edition, with an addenda.
224 pp.   New York."

The same.   Second Edition with an addenda of 23
pages.   New York.

CATALOGUE of the Coins and Medals, Ancient and Modern, belonging to the New York State Library. Prepared by request
by Richard W. Davids, Esq., of Philadelphia.   58 pp.   8vo.
                                                 Albany.   1853.

1854.

CATALOGUE of the extraordinary curiosities in the National Institute and Patent Office.   Washington.   by Alfred Hunter.
74 pp.   8vo.   Washington.   1854.

CATALOGUE of Coins (Duplicates) Ancient and Modern, in the
possession of the New York State Library.
               (189 Lots).   4 pp.   8vo.   Albany.   1854.

CATALOGUE of the Coins, Ancient and Modern, belonging to the
New York State Library. Prepared by request, by Richard
W. Davids Esq., of Philadelphia. 62 pp. 8vo. Albany. 1854.

The last four pages describe the duplicates, which are the same as those
described in the preceding catalogue.

CATALOGUE of the Manuscripts, Maps, Medals, Coins .... of the
Maryland Historical Society, by Lewis Mayer. 51 pp. 8vo.
Baltimore. 1854.

On pp. 40 to 45 is a partial descriptive list of coins, belonging to the Society.

1855.

CHAMBERS, HARMON A. A Catalogue of rare and valuable
Coins, Medals, Minerals, Fossils, Corals, Shells, Manuscripts,
Antiquities, Curiosities. Collected and arranged by Harmon
A. Chambers. 23 pp. 8vo. Carbondale, Penn. 1855.

CATALOGUE of the Extraordinary Curiosities in the National Institute and Patent Office. by Alfred Hunter. 2d Edition.
70 pp. 8vo. Washington. 1855.

" Prof. D. E. GROUX's Museum of Antiquities. A card 3x4½
inches. Illustrated. On which is printed an offer to purchase, sell, or exchange a large number of things at No. 265
Washington Street. No date. Boston.

CATALOGUE of Medal and Coins. For the disposal of the best
collection of Medals, Coins, and Numismatical Works in the
United States. Catalogue of a Grand Collection of Coins
and Medals .... etc. Daniel E. Groux. Dec. 1st, 1855.
16mo. 16pp. Boston. 1855.

The copy before me also has in addition a "Circular" of the same date
explanatory of the reason for disposing of his collection (D. E. Groux's) by a
lottery.

Under the date of the 20th December 1855 he published another small circular, headed:

"Additional Arrangements made for the interest of the Ticket Holders,"

In which he pledges himself, not to sell more than 450 Tickets (@ $10.00), and announcing the appointment of Dr. Winslow Lewis and Joseph M. Wightman as Trustees, and of Mr. N. D. Hubbard as Treasurer. The 2d page is blank, on the 3d is a selection of "Names from Dec. 1st to the 15th."

In a letter from a friend, he informs me that he has a manuscript "Catalogue of Coins, Medals, &c." prepared for him by Mr. Groux, Oct. 17th 1845, containing some 8291 pieces. This is probably the first catalogue of Mr. Groux's collection.

CATALOGUE of the New York State Library.
3 vol.   Royal 8vo.   Albany.   1855 and 1857.

The 1st and 2d volumes of this catalogue are books only and bear the imprint of 1855, the 3d Vol. appears not to have been printed until 1857, which is the one containing the list of " Maps Manuscripts Engravings Coins &c."

1856.

CATALOGUE of the Medals, Coins, Paper Money, etc., in the New York State Library 1856.   The Pages are numbered 147 to 212.   66 pp.   8vo.   Albany.   1857.

This is evidently a separate publication of a portion of the 3d vol. of the State Library catalogue. See also under date of 1857.

"D"   CATALOGUE of the Coins and Medals, Ancient and Modern. Belonging to the New York State Library. Prepared by request, by Richard W. Davids Esq., of Philadelphia. The pages are numbered 167 @ 222. A fragment from "Assembly Documents" No. 138.

CATALOGUE   C. H. MORSE

Offered for sale by Mr. Woodward in his list of Coin catalogues published March 15th 1864. Not having seen a copy of it, can give no further particulars.

1857.

CATALOGUE of Autographs, and coins (on p. 15) for sale by Charles B. Norton. (With printed prices.) 16pp. New York.

CATALOGUE of the Medals, Coins, Paper Money, etc., in the New
   York State Library: 1856.   Albany.   1857.
   (pp. numbered 147 to 212.   8vo.)
   This is a portion separately bound of the following volume.

CATALOGUE of the New York State Library 1856. Maps, Manuscripts, Engravings, Coins, etc. (274 pp. 8vo.) Albany 1857.
   This forms the third volume of the Catalogue of the Library, the first two being
   issued in 1856.

CATALOGUE of the Curiosities in the National Institute and in
   the Patent Office.   Washington.   71 pp.   8vo.   (2d Edition.)
                                               Washington.   1857.

1858.

PRICED CATALOGUE of Coins, Medals, and Numismatic Works of
   all Nations, for sale by John K. Curtis. (18 pp. 8vo.) New York.

PRICED CATALOGUE.
   Henry Whipple & Son.   (11 pp. sm. 4to.) Salem. (Mass.)

CATALOGUE of the Collection of Curiosities at Washington Head-
   Quarters.   Newburgh, N. Y.

CATALOGUE of the Massachusetts State Library.   Boston.
   (Medals on pp. 276 and 277)

1859.

PRICED CATALOGUE of Coins, Medals, etc. For Sale by John K.
   Curtis.   (42 pp.   8vo.)   New York.

CATALOGUE of Coins, Medals, and Tokens of all nations in Gold,
   Silver and Copper, for sale by Augustus B. Sage. February
   1859.   " No. 1 " Price 10 cents.   New York.
   (8 pp. 8vo.   Illustrated.)

—— " No. 2."   New York.
   A reprint; with illustrations in reverse order, the N. E. Shilling being at the top,
   and " Price 25 cents."

Priced Catalogue of Autographs, Minerals, Coins, Medals for
sale by C. H. Morse, Cambridgeport, Mass., and 16 State St.,
Boston.

23 pp. 4to—in which are offered in double columns about 2000 lots.

Catalogue of Coins Medals & Tokens, Autographs, Old Books
&c. for sale by A. B. Sage & Co. June 1859. Price 25 Cents.
(24 pp.   8vo.)   New York.

A Popular Catalogue of the Extraordinary Curiosities in the
National Institute arranged in the building belonging to the
Patent Office.   Washington. 1859.
Published by Alfred Hunter.   48 pp. 8vo.

An Illustrated Catalogue and Guide Book.   Barnum's
American Museum.   New York.

The following is an interesting squib, published at that time in the form of a
note size circular, which though not entitled to a place here, yet on account of
the sound spirit pervading it, it deserves more than an ephemeral existence.

"Philadelphia, October   1859.

COIN COLLECTORS, TO THE RESCUE!

THE CAROLINA ELEPHANT IN THE FIELD!!

Whereas, certain parties in the City of Brotherly Love have combined together
to furnish the inhabitants of Philadelphia with Counterfeit Washington Cents, and
½ Dollars, (the Lord Baltimore Coinage) also the Sommer Island Shilling, or Hog
Cent :

We, the Coin Collectors of Philadelphia, seeing the impropriety of the above,
have agreed not to purchase any of the above-mentioned pieces, or any that may
be made as Copies of Rare Coins or Medals, from this date.

There have been several attempts made to re-strike rare coins within the last year
or two, and it is high time that a stop should be put to it.

On some of the above pieces the word copy has been made, but in so slight a
manner as to be easily erased, and then you cannot tell them from the genuine.

We would especially call the attention of the curious Public to the Sommer
Island, or Hog Cent, without the word copy, (but instead, the word Root
or Die.

We say, Die—Die—Die.

Probably Viator, alias George H. Hickorynuts, has something to do with the re-
striking of those Pieces.

We remain your most humble servants,

TIMOTHY ANTIQUARY,
JULIUS CÆSAR,
Dr. TIMBERCRACKS, M. D., L. L. D.

(L. L. D. means Long Legged Devil.)

1860.

CATALOGUE of Coins Medals and Tokens of all Nations for sale
by Wm. H. Dayton. 73 Bleecker Street N. Y. Catalogue
Twenty Five Cents. (50 pp. 8vo.)   New York.

NORTONS Literary Letter No. 1. New Series. (Contains a
priced list of coins for sale.) (45 pp. 4to.)   New York.
      The "Letter No. 2" contains nothing relating to coins.

"List of Medal Dies of a Public Character in the Mint of the
United States" contains a price list of the medals. 2 pages
Letter size, with date 186 ....   Philadelphia.

"ANCIENT AND MODERN COINS for sale" by B. Homans.
                                              New York.
    A circular in letter form offering a collection of "1500 and 1600 coins for sale."

1861.

CURTIS, JOHN K. "To Numismatists in Particular! And to
everybody in general! The greatest chance ever offered to
obtain rare and valuable Coins and Medals, at the very low
sum of one dollar each."   New York.
      (A lottery scheme) describing coins. Printed on a single sheet about 6x9 inches.

ROBINSON, A. S. "Catalogue of a choice and valuable collection of Gold Silver and Copper Coins **** for sale by
Alfred S. Robinson *** For terms of sale see Third page
of cover." (A Lottery scheme.) (502 lots. 16 pp. 8vo.)
                               Hartford. June 25th 1861.

PRICED CATALOGUE of Coins and Medals for sale by Alfred S.
Robinson. Marble Block. Hartford. (16 pp. 16mo.)
                               Hartford. July 1, 1861.

"COINS" For sale by Benjamin Hill. (Cents and Half Cents.)
(The 1st page has only the word "Coins") (3 pp. small 4to.)
                                              Philadelphia.

HARPEL, OSCAR H. Catalogue of Books Coins Medals &c. for
sale by—cor. 3d and Vine Sts. (22 pp. 8vo.)   Cincinnati.

CATALOGUE of a Choice and Valuable Collection of American and Foreign Silver and Copper Coins, Medals &c. **** It is the property of a private collector.   Philadelphia.

This was the C. DE HAVEN collection which was disposed of at private sale through Mr. Edward Cogan to Mr. William A. Lilliendahl. The copy in my possession has the respective valuation by each of the above named gentlemen placed on each side of the page opposite each piece, except in some instances where the pieces were not taken or were sold in a lot.

SAGE, A. B. & Co. "To Coin Collectors." A Lottery scheme circular, dated March 1, 1861. Drawing on and after March 5th, 1861. 1 pp.   New York.

1862.

○ CURTIS, JOHN K.   Catalogue of Coins Medals etc. for sale by (31 pp.   Large 8vo.)   New York.

MÜLLER, CHARLES. "Description of the Sumter and Pickens Medals," (with price list. 2 pp. Letter size.) New York.

ROHAN, EDWARD.   Price List of coins.   12 Brattle Square. (Printed on a note sheet. 2 pp. 8vo.)   Boston.

"LIST of Medal Dies of a Public Character in the Mint of the United States, from which Medals will be struck, at the annexed rates, to societies and individuals who may apply for the same." (4 pp. 4to.) October 1862.   Philadelphia.

McCOY, A. R. "American Coins and Medals Wanted" (A circular note size with prices of coins. 1 page.) Dated Jan. 20 1862.   Easton. Penn.

This little circular introduces to us Mr. A. Ramsay McCoy, a gentleman, now a resident of Orange, N. J. and engaged in the leather trade in the "Swamp", in this city, who has unostentatiously and quietly formed a cabinet of the "Political Medals," which is probably without an equal in this country, in addition to which he has also a collection of the Mint issues, copper and silver of a choice character. He has also a fine collection of coin catalogues. Not quite as generally known as his brother John F., but equally courteous and affable, rather retiring and unobstrusive, he must be sought like a hidden violet. As a numismatist his knowledge in his specialty is probably unexcelled by any one, disposing of nothing until he has obtained a better, his cabinet has been constantly improving, and with no idea of relinquishing his collection during his life, in vain may others hope to have the opportunity of a bid at his "*uniques*," for which opportunity may they have to wait for many years. Messrs. John F. and A. Ramsay McCoy are both natives of Pennsylvania.

Woodward, W. E. In a Circular, dated June 3d 1862, this gentleman offers :

> The "Harrison Jubilee Medal" and Bolen's "U. S. A." or "Bar Cent."

—— "A Table giving the year of coinage of all American Coins and the prices at which I will purchase them" also a "Table giving brief descriptions of rare American Coins" with "Remarks." (4 pp. 4to.)   Roxbury. 1862.

Gerdts, Henry D. "Numismatic Hall" "Coin Emporium." (A sheet note size.)   May. New York. 1862.

1863.

Catalogue of the Cabinet of Coins belonging to YALE COL-LEGE. Illustrated with a fac-simile of the N. E. Three-pence, in its possession. (48 pp. 8vo.)   New Haven. 1863.

> A serviceable catalogue to a numismatist. The following extract states the position of the college. "*We shall be glad to receive any donations, and each piece will be recorded with the name of the donor. Any one desiring of helping us can bring or send donations to the College Library, where they will be taken care of. Lately a few dollars each year have been expended, by vote of the Corporation, when a good opportunity has offered, principally upon ancient coins, but the college must depend mainly on free-will offerings, as there is no fund for the purpose.*" The italicizing is my work, for the purpose of calling attention to an excellent place for some of our wealthy collectors to dispose of some of their fine duplicates "where they will do the most good," that is in "training the young idea how to shoot." While upon this subject, I would also suggest another place to send duplicates, that is to the "FREE COLLEGE OF THE CITY OF NEW YORK," where that skilled numismatist Prof. Charles E. Anthon, will see that they are well taken care of, and usefully employed.

Woodward, W. E. Roxbury, May 30, 1863. "Priced Catalogues of my recent sale in New York are now ready. **** One or more copies each of the following Catalogues, can be supplied at the prices annexed."

> Then follows a list of thirty catalogues with prices asked.
>
> This, although not a coin catalogue, is considered germane to the general subject, and is therefore given a place here. It is a single sheet on note paper.

Woodward, W. E. Boston June 30, 1863.

> A List of coin catalogues printed on a single letter sheet.

BISHOP, E.   A Circular note form in which he offers for sale
Medals struck from dies by Morin and Paquet. "Obv. Head
of Washington.   Rev. Crystal Palace in New York."
This is the only relic of this once well-known numismatist.

BENNET, CHARLES E.   162 Vine St.   Price List of coins for
sale by—   Cincinnati O. 1863.
   175 lots.   8 pp.   small 8vo.

1864.

"CATALOGUE of Coins of Mrs. Marshall, Hobart, N. Y.   For
sale at . . . . . . " (9 pp.   8vo.)   1864.

CATALOGUE of the Museum of Flags, Trophies, and Relics,
relating to the Revolution, the War of 1812.   The Mexican
War and the present Rebellion forming the most complete
and interesting Collection ever brought together in the United
States : To be exhibited at New York, April 4, 1864, and on
the succeeding days for the benefit of the United States
Sanitary Commission. (110 pp.   8vo.)   New York.   1864.

WOODWARD, W. E.   Circular announcing the "McCoy Collection" for sale.   On the second and third pages is a "List
of Catalogues which I am now able to furnish," with the
prices of each.   Roxbury, Mass. March 15th, 1864.
   A letter sheet.   3 pp.   4to.

COOK, HENRY.   " Coin Catalogue."   74 Friend St., Boston.
   A single letter sheet.

BULKLEY, C. A.   " Price List of coins" for sale by C. A. Bulkley, Granville. Washington Co.   New York.
   A single sheet, 7x13 inches.

BENNET, CHAS. E.   Price List of Coins.   (348 Lots.)
                                           Cincinnati O. 1864.

"CATALOGUE of Arts Relics and Curiosities on exhibition at
the Taylor House cor. Taylor and Montague Sts."   For the
benefit of the United States Sanitary Commission.   Feb. 22d.
                                           Brooklyn.   1864.

Thompson Bros. Coin Chart Manual. Published by D. Hawes, 22 Beekman St. (48 pp. 4to.) New York. 1864.

Upon Mr. Hawes taking charge of the publication of this manual, he added three plates of illustrations. It has been thus issued yearly since then.

1865.

Yale College. Catalogue of Ancient Coins added to the Yale College Collection Aug. 1863—Feb. 1865. (4 pp. 8vo.) New Haven. 1865.

Gointoem Strong. "Supplementary Catalogue of a Collection of Coins and Medals gathered from half a dozen worthless collections, now the property of Gointoem Strong Esq. to be sold this day. Smoked Glass will be provided for those who wish to examine the coins." 3 pp. small note size, describing some 16 lots.

This catalogue was the production of Mr. Charles Chaplin of Charlestown District, Boston, Mass., a prominent numismatist, one of the most active members of the Boston Numismatic Society, and at the same time one of the more modest and retiring. Those who have not the good fortune to possess a copy of the catalogue, are referred to Vol. IV. p. 7 of the "American Journal of Numismatics," where it has been deservedly honored with a less perishable form for its wit and lively sense of the ludicrous. On page 8 of the same volume may be found a "*pome*" from the same pen, but which was furnished to that journal by another gentleman, whose full initials are "S. S. C."

By some it was thought (erroneously, however) that the squib was written with "malice prepense" to satirize the descriptive coin catalogues of other parties. The following explanation will elucidate the history of its origin and "*raison d'être.*"—Mr. Chaplin's vocation is that of a printer; one day, while his workmen were at dinner, he availed himself of a few leisure moments, numismatist-like, to look over some old coins, the refuse of a recent purchase, which were in his desk, it was such a "very poor" lot that it so strongly excited his sense of the ridiculous, that he was impelled to at once take up a "composing stick" and catalogue the collection from sight, and without "copy," with the result shown in the catalogue. Lot "16" records an incident, which those accustomed to attending auction sales have undoubtedly seen similar instances occur. "An old Half Dime of a numismatic value of about ten or fifteen cents was put up for bids, none were offered, after some delay, the auctioneer said in a jocose way, "Who will give five dollars for this nice coin?" "I will!" said an innocent by-stander, and instanter the coin was knocked down to him.

VAIL, JOHN COOPER. "Washington Market Newspaper and Literary Depot. Peoples Hotel, 106 Vesey Street, New York." "To Numismatologists, 2000 rare American and English coins all genuine, no fac-similes."
4 pp. 8vo. (no date.)   New York.

> This price-list and circular, in which this errant and versatile genius offers to sell coins, write poems, obituaries, patriotic speeches, epitaphs, love-letters, etc., as well as to teach lightning calculation, elocution, and theatricals, was issued about 1865 or 1866.

1866.

DEAKIN, WALTER A. Priced Catalogue of Coins, etc., for sale by ––––, 336 Clark St. (614 lots, 20 pp. 8vo.)
                                            Chicago, 1866.

WARNER, JOHN S. & SONS. "Centenary Medals." To commemorate the Centennial Anniversary of the Methodist Episcopal Church in the United States. (1 p. letter size.) 326 Chestnut St.   Philadelphia.

UNITED STATES MINT, Phia. Price List of Medals, etc. (12 pp. 8vo.)   July 1st. Philadelphia.

MASON BROTHERS (GEO. B. and J. ALLAN MASON) 59 Liberty Street. (A circular in which they offer Coins, Curiosities, &c. Single sheet, note size.)   New York, 1866.

BULKLEY, C. A. "Price list of Coins for 186–."
                                            Granville, N. Y.
> Gives dates of U. S. Cents, but not prices.

"MINT OF THE UNITED STATES." Circular letter in relation to American Medals and Cabinet Coins. Henry R. Lindemann, Director. (12 pp., 12mo.)   Philadelphia, July 1, 1866.

1867.

MASON & Co. New and Improved Priced Coin Catalogue for 1867. 14th Edition. (4 pp.)   Philadelphia.

1868.

E. MASON JR. "Mason's Coin Priced Catalogue for 1868, showing prices paid by Coin Dealers for American and Foreign Coins. when in good condition. Improved and corrected semi-annually. Price 25 cents." Published by Mason & Wells, No. 50 North Tenth street. 12 pp. 12mo.

Philadelphia.

1869.

EDWARD COGAN. "To Collectors." A circular giving description and prices of "The Johnson Medalet."
(Single note sheet.) March 1869, New York.

SIMS, J. R. Catalogue of the private cabinet of J. R. Sims, Fort Plain, N. Y. 1869.
(380 lots. 34 pp. 8vo. Sold at private sale).

WARNER, WILLIAM H. & BROTHER. "Odd Fellow's Anniversary Medal," "General U. S. Grant." (Two circulars printed in blue ink, offering the above medals for sale.)
728 Chestnut St. Philadelphia.

WARNER, CHAS. K. "Medal of Joseph J. Mickley, Esq."
326 Chestnut Street. Philadelphia.
Descriptive price list, single sheet, note size.

U. S. MINT. "Pacific Railway Medal." Philadelphia, 1869.
A descriptive price list, 3 pp. 8vo.

1870.

Catalogue of Alaskan Antiquities and Curiosities, now on exhibition at the Clinton Hall Art Galleries, Astor Place and 8th Street. Leavitt, Strebeigh & Co. Price of Catalogue, 25 cents. (32 pp. 8vo.) New York.

This collection, the property of Edward G. Fast, Esq., late of the U. S. Army, was made by him while stationed in Alaska; it was exhibited here, and shortly after disposed of to Prof. Agassiz of Harvard College. The catalogues were all destroyed, as supposed, but a very few copies exist in the hands of coin catalogue collectors.

MASON & Co's Coin Priced Circular, containing a list of coins, etc., on hand and for sale by Mason & Co., Coin and Stamp Dealers, 139 N. Ninth Street, Philadelphia. (3 pp. 4to.)
Philadelphia. 1870.

COGAN, E. "To the Alumni, Students and Friends of Haverford College." New York.
> A single sheet, letter size, describing and offering for sale the well-known "Haverford College Medal."

COGAN, E. "Norwalk Washington Medal." New York.
> Another circular from Mr. Cogan, describing and offering the above-named medal. A single sheet, letter size.

E. MASON, JR. "Improved Coin Priced Catalogue for 1870. 16 pp. Philadelphia. 1870.

MASON & Co. "Price current of a Private Collection," with prices of each piece. (92 lots. 4 pp. note size.) Philadelphia.

1871.

MASON's Improved Coin Priced Catalogue for 1871. Showing the prices paid by Coin Dealers for American and Foreign Coins. Prepared for the use of Brokers, Storekeepers and Collectors by E. Mason Jr., Numismatist. Price 25 cents. (16 pp. 16mo.) Philadelphia. 1871.
> Mr. Mason or the Publishers in the "Explanatory Preface" make an erroneous statement (as may be readily seen by looking back to the years 1858 and 1859,) when they assert that "Having published in 1860 the first Coin Priced Catalogue ever issued in the United States." I am willing to admit that I have not yet seen a "Coin Priced Catalogue" published by Mr. Mason in 1860. Who has?

CATALOGUE of Coins, Medals, &c., in stock and for sale by Mason & Co., 139 North Ninth St. Price 25 cents. (20 pp. 8vo.) Philadelphia. 1871.

SCOTT & Co., J. W. "Coin Priced Catalogue showing the fictitious value of all American coin, prepared for the use of Collectors, Brokers and Storekeepers. Price 25 cents. J. W. Scott & Co., 75 & 77 Nassau St. (16 pp. 8vo.)
New York. 1871.

H. G. SAMPSON, Broadway corner of Fulton street, New York.

This catalogue appears to be the same as the last described, with their name and place of business erased and that of Mr Sampson inserted.

1872.

HASELTINE, JOHN W. Catalogue of United States and Foreign Coins, Medals, &c., for sale by John W. Haseltine, No. 512 Walnut Street, Philadelphia, 1872 & 1873. (32 pp. 8vo.)
Philadelphia.

Mr. Haseltine, under the date of July 1st, 1872, made his bow to the numismatic public; he has since offered at public sale quite a number of collections which were placed in his hands for such disposition; he subsequently removed to No. 1225 Chestnut Street, where he is still ready to serve his friends and the public generally.

WATSON & Co. Priced Catalogue of Coins, Medals, Paper Money, &c., 139 N. Ninth St., Philadelphia. Price 25 cents.
Philadelphia.

SANDERS, ALFRED. Catalogue of Coins, Silver and Copper, and Medals of various countries, contained in the cabinet of Alfred Sanders, Dec'd, late of Davenport, Iowa. (16 pp. 8vo.)
Davenport, Iowa, 1872.

This collection of 1290 coins was disposed of at private sale by Mrs. A. Sanders.

COGAN, EDWARD. "New Wyon Medal." National thanksgiving for recovery of the Prince of Wales, Feb. 1872. (A circular and price list, letter size.) Brooklyn, 1872.

KLINE, JOHN W. "Established 1857. Price List of Medals for sale by John W. Kline, No. 212 South Eighth Street, Philadelphia, Pa." (4 pp. 4to size, illustrated.)

KLINE, JOHN W. "Campaign Medals for 1872." (A Price list on a half letter sheet. 1 page.) Philadelphia.

BULKLEY, C. A. "Reduced Price List of Coin Packets for sale by C. A. Bulkley, Granville, Washington Co., N. Y." (Single Sheet, 7½x6½.)

The various lots are numbered 1 to 64, with prices to each.

BULKLEY, C. A. "Reduced Price List of Coin Packets for sale by C. A. Bulkley,   Granville, Washington Co., N. Y. (Single Sheet, 7½x6⅓.)

> The various lots are numbered 65 to 137, with prices to each, a casual glance might mislead, as the head of each price list is printed with the same type and in the same style but the numbering of the lots differs.

SCRIBNER, WELFORD & ARMSTRONG. "Holiday List of Books." (84 pp. 8vo.)   New York. 1872.

> On page 62 of this list of Books for sale, appears the following strayer:
> "Napoleon Medals in bronze, in a morocco case, ten kinds, very fine, very scarce, $15.00."

MINT OF THE UNITED STATES. "Circular letter in relation to American Medals and Cabinet Coins. James Pollock, Director." (2 pp. Letter size.)   Philadelphia. 1872.

1873.

CATALOGUE of a small collection of Paintings, Miniatures, Antiquities, &c., recently brought from Europe by an English Artist, including a fine original Picture by Benjamin West. 709 Broadway. First floor up stairs, front. Open from 10 A. M. to 6 P. M. (7 pp. 8vo.)   New York.

> The lots are not numbered. On page 5 the 12th lot from the top is described as a "Set of Scientific Medals in case." The same lot afterwards sold by Messrs. Leavitt, Nov. 10, 1873. q. v.

MINT OF THE UNITED STATES. "Circular Letter in relation to American Medals and Cabinet Coins," with price list. (2 pp. Letter size.)   Philadelphia. 1873.

BULKLEY, C. A. "Catalogue of Coins for Sale by C. A. Bulkley,   Granville, Washington Co., N. Y.
The text in one column.
A single sheet, 6 x7½ inches, the lots are numbered 138 to 174.

BULKLEY, C. A. "Price List of Foreign Coins for Sale by C. A. Bulkley,   Granville, Washington Co., N. Y."

> A single sheet, 7¼x 9 inches, two columns. Lots numbered 176 to 285. It may be noticed that the next priced catalogue of Mr. Bulkley commences with the number 470. He informs me that he issued no price list in which are the intervening numbers.

1874.

SPENCER, A. H.   Price list of Foreign Coins, for sale by A. H.
Spencer,   East Clarendon, Vt.
   A sheet 6½x11 in., 81 lots, 2 columns.

SCOTT & Co., J. W.   Catalogue of American & Foreign copper coin, with the prices at which they can be purchased of
the publishers.   Illustrated.   Published by J. W. Scott &
Co., 75 & 77 Nassau Street, New York City."
(16 pp. 8vo, no date, but issued in 1874.)

HILL, JAMES L.   Catalogue of Coins and Medals Ancient and
Modern, prepared by James D. Butler, LL. D., and D. S.
Durrie, Esq., from the collection of James L. Hill, Esq., Late
Mayor of the City, and President of the late Bank of Madi-
son.   (18 pp. 8vo.)   Madison, Wis.
   This collection was sold to Mr. F. Haines of Biddeford, Maine.

KLINE, JOHN W.   Priced Catalogue.   Philadelphia.
(8 pp.)

BULKLEY, C. A.   " Established in 1860.   Catalogue of Miscellaneous Coins, sold by C. A. Bulkley.
                        Granville, Washington County, N. Y."
   A sheet 7½x11, in two columns.   Lots numbered 470 to 554.

BULKLEY, C. A.   "Established in 1860.   Catalogue of Coins
and Cards for sale by C. A. Bulkley,
                         Granville, Washington County, N. Y."
   A sheet 7½ by 14, in lots not numbered.

HASELTINE, JOHN W.   A circular, note size, in which he describes and offers for sale the Thiers medal.   Philadelphia.
HASELTINE, JOHN W., and Randall, J. C.   " Circular to Collectors."   Philadelphia.   1874.
   In which they announce the " discovering" and purchasing the dies of the Confederate Cent, or some other "mare's nest" of the kind, and offering the coins
for sale.

MERCER, R. W.   "Coin Price List."   Cincinnati, O.
   A sheet, note size.

COGAN, EDWARD.   A circular, note size, in which he offers for
sale the "Boston Numismatic and New England Historic-
Genealogical Societies" Medal.

CATALOGUE of the Collection of Arms, Armor and other subjects loaned to the Metropolitan Museum of Art by H. Cogniat Esq.   (603 lots.   29 pp.   8vo.)   New York.   1874.

1875.

CATALOGUE of the Collection of Arms, Armor and other objects, loaned to the Metropolitan Museum of Art.   New
York, by H. Cogniat Esq.   New York.   1875.
(655 lots.   25 pp.   8vo.)

SCOTT & Co., J. W.   Catalogue of American & Foreign Silver
Coin with the prices at which they can be purchased of the
publishers.   Illustrated.   Price 50 cents.   Published by
J. W. Scott & Co. 75 & 77 Nassau Street, New York City.
   A finely illustrated catalogue of 16 pages.   8vo.

SCOTT & Co., J. W.   "The American Journal of Philately."
                                               New York.   1875.
   In several numbers of this Journal they have inserted a supplement which
gives "Philatelic & Numismatic Announcements" with illustrations.   The pages
of the supplement are numbered III to XVIII.   16 pp.   8vo.

SCOTT & Co., J. W.   "Philatelic & Numismatic Circular for
1876."
   This is a cover illustrated, and used by that firm to place over the above supplement and also on the following as may suit their convenience.

SCOTT & Co., J. W.   "Announcements, Philatelic and Numismatic."   (8 pages.   8vo.   No date.)   New York.

" J. F. W." (Wood).   "Centennio-Satirical Medal."
                                          New York.   July 3d 1873.
   In this two page letter size circular this gentleman sharply rebukes the American
people for their passiveness and inaction in not completing the Washington
Monument at the Capitol of the U. S.; after the conclusion of the letter follows a
description of a medal with the names of the persons from whom it can be obtained.

ABBEY, LORENZO H.   Price List of United States Copper Cents
for sale by L. H. Abbey.   Box 23.   South Orange, N. J.   1875.
   A small sheet.

BULKLEY, C. A. "The Oldest Coin House in the U. S. Established in 1860. List of Foreign Copper Coins for sale by C. A. Bulkley, Granville, Washington Co., N. Y."
A 7½x9 sheet.

BULKLEY, C. A. "Established in 1860. Price List of U. S. Cents for sale by C. A. Bulkley, Granville, Washington Co., N. Y."
A 4x7 sheet.

BULKLEY, C. A. "List of Packets of Coins for sale by C. A. Bulkley, Granville, Washington Co., N. Y."
A 4x4½ sheet.

HOLWAY, EDWARD W. "Catalogue of Coins, Medals, and Numismatic Works for sale by Edward W. Holway, (3 pp. 8vo.) Decorah, Iowa."

SPENCER, A. H. "List of Coins, Minerals, Chromos, Curiosities, &c., for sale by A. H. Spencer, East Clarendon, Rutland Co., Vt."
A little pamphlet, 8 pp., 3x6 inches.

PROSKEY, DAVID. A little circular announcing for sale a "Centennial Medal, commemorating the visit to Boston of the 7th Reg't N. G. of New York.
Mr. Proskey is now at No. 186 Washington St., New York.

AUSTIN, JAMES M. A note circular giving an illustration of the "Dedication Medal" adopted by the trustees of the Masonic Hall and Asylum Fund, and of the price, &c. New York.

BOYSEN, L. Price list of Coins for sale by L. Boysen, 165 Genesee Street, Buffalo, N. Y.
A sheet 5x8, printed on both sides.

AHLBORN, HENRY. "Catalogue of American and Foreign Coins Wanted by Henry Ahlborn, at the "Old Toll House," foot of Cambridge St., Boston, Mass."
A sheet 6½x7½.

ENTERPRISE STAMP CO. "Price list of Coins for sale by Enterprise Stamp Co. P. B. 107 Station A. Cleveland, O.
A 5x8 sheet.

MERCER, R. W. " Retail Price List American Copper Cents
and Half Cents. Mercer's Stencil House, 117 West Sixth
Street,   .   Cincinnati, O.
A sheet 5x8 inches.

MERCER, R. W. " Coin Price List." 148 Main Street, S. E.
Cor. of Fourth.   Cincinnati, O.
Note size. .

SELLON, ED. M. " Solicitor for the sale of American, Foreign
and Ancient Gold, Silver and Copper Coins and Medals.
P. O. Drawer 44.   Castile, Wyoming County. N. Y."
A sheet 5x13 inches.

DILLINGHAM, GEO. A. "Catalogue of Coins and Medals for sale
by George A. Dillingham.   Titusville, Penn."
(59 lots, Note form.)

BISHOP, C. L. " Rare American Coins of different dates and
denominations."   Jamestown, N. Y.
A little slip about an inch in width and 5 inches in length.

LOCKWOOD & HERRING. " Price List of United States Cop-
pers."   440 E. Houston Street,   New York.
A single sheet, note size.

HASELTINE, JOHN W. " Catalogue of United States and Foreign Coins, Medals, &c. For sale by John W. Haseltine,
No. 1225 Chestnut Street, Philadelphia. Price Twenty-Five
cents. (56 pp. 8vo.)   Philadelphia, 1875.

HASELTINE, JOHN W. " Priced Coin Catalogues, for sale by
John W. Haseltine, No. 1225 Chestnut Street.
(4 pp. 8vo.)   Philadelphia, 1875.

HASELTINE, JOHN W. " Centennial Medals for sale by John
W. Haseltine, No 1225 Chestnut Street."   Philadelphia.
(Single sheet, no date).

HASELTINE, JOHN W. " Centennial Continental Dollar designed
by Benjamin Franklin." (Note sheet, no date.) Philadelphia.

HASELTINE, JOHN W. " Fac-Simile of the Centennial Medal.
The Memorial Medals of the Centennial of 1876."
(Sheet 6x12, no date).   Philadelphia.

HASELTINE, JOHN W. "Centennial. The following Medals which I offer for sale are patented." (Sheet 6x9, no date).
Philadelphia.

HASELTINE, JOHN W. "Centennio-Satirical Washington Medal." (Note sheet, no date). Philadelphia.

HASELTINE, JOHN W. "The accompanying Engraving is a facsimile of the Centennial Medal which we desire to present to your notice." (Sheet 8x9½, no date.) Philadelphia.

Illustrated with obverse and reverse of the "Main Building" and "Art Gallery."

"CENTENNIAL MEDALS carved in solid walnut."

A photographic plate illustrating obverses of six medals.
A sheet, note size, the bottom of which appears to have been cut off. Mr. John W. Haseltine has a little slip pasted on the upper part of the sheet with his name and address.

HASELTINE, JOHN W. "Memorial of a Century, 1776, 1876." Philadelphia.

Illustrations of "Independence" and "Memorial Halls," a sheet, letter size.

DOUGLAS, WILLIAM. "Catalogue of U. S. and Foreign Coins for sale by." (8 pp. 8vo.) Zanesville, Ohio.

PARKER, T. M. "Catalogue of United States and Foreign Coins and Fine Medals for sale by." (12 pp. 12mo.)
Woburn, Mass.

PARKER, T. M. "Coins." "The following lots of U. S. Coins are offered for sale," etc. Woburn, Mass.

Printed on a slip 4x11 inches.

DOUGLAS, JR., WM. A Price List of Foreign and U. S. Coins.
Lanesville, Ohio.

A note size sheet. By some error this is printed *Lanesville* instead of *Zanesville*. Ohio.

FIFTH CATALOGUE of the Collection of Ancient and Modern Works of Art, given or loaned to the Trustees of the Museum of Fine Arts at Boston, now on Exhibition in the Public Gallery of the Athenæum. (75 pp. 8vo.) Boston. 1875.

On p. 58 is a "Gold Medal," etc.

PART III

Publications issued in the United States.

— •••—

The following is a partial list of works printed in this country which describe, illustrate, or allude to Coins or Medals, or subjects germane. In giving this list it is only intended to illustrate the varied sources from which numismatic knowledge and information may be derived, and serve as a hint in the formation of a numismatic library. In the daily papers are frequently articles of importance, which may be cut out and pasted in a scrap book, to which a suitable "INDEX" of subjects should be kept.

ALDEN. T. Collections of American Epitaphs. 5 Vols. 12mo.
New York. 1814.

AMERICAN Academy of Arts and Sciences.
(Memoirs, Vol. III., Part 1. See pp. 195 and 196.)

AMERICAN Encyclopedia. (7 vols. 8vo.) New York. 1806.

AMERICAN Historical and Literary Curiosities. (4to.)
Philadelphia. 1847.

"AMERICAN JOURNAL OF NUMISMATICS and BULLETIN of the AMERICAN NUMISMATIC and ARCHÆOLOGICAL SOCIETY."
New York and Boston.

This valuable publication was commenced and issued under the auspices of the above-named Society in May, 1866, but though not a success when looked at from a pecuniary point of view, yet it continued its monthly appearance for four years, when the responsibility of its publication was transferred from the New York Society to that of the "BOSTON NUMISMATIC SOCIETY," who changed it from a monthly to a quarterly; as such it still flourishes.

AMERICAN MUSEUM. 8vo. Philadelphia. 1789.
(See Vol. II. p. 403.)

AMERICAN NUMISMATIC and ARCHÆOLOGICAL SOCIETY—Constitution and By-Laws of. Founded 1857. (12 pp. 8vo.)
New York. 1864.

AMERICAN NUMISMATIC and ARCHÆOLOGICAL SOCIETY—Articles of Incorporation, Constitution and By-Laws. (18 pp. 8vo.)
New York. 1865.

"AMERICAN STAMP MERCURY and NUMISMATIST." Boston.

This was a monthly publication issued by Messrs. Trifet & Co. of Boston. It made its bow to the public in 1867, as the "AMERICAN STAMP MERCURY." After a year's time, "and NUMISMATIST" was added to its title; in August, 1870, they announced that "we have this month struck the 'Numismatist' for ever." In March 1871 it ceased to exist, 39 numbers, comprising 388 pages, having been issued.

AMERICAN STATE PAPERS. (7 vols. Folio.) Washington. 1832-34.
See Vol I. pp. 14-19. Vol. VII. pp. 91-107.

ANNUAL REPORT of the Directors of the UNITED STATES' MINT.
Philadelphia.
Published various dates.

ANNUAL REPORT of the Trustees of the New York State Library.
(222 pp. 8vo.) Albany. 1854.
Vide pp. 65 and 122.

ANNUAL REPORT of the Trustees of the New York State Library. Albany. 1855.
(Vide pp. 63, 74, 84, 85.)

ANTHON, CHARLES E. Historical Cabinet of the College of the City of New York. (15 pp. 8vo.) New York. 1874.

APPLETON'S ENCYCLOPÆDIA. (16 vols. 8vo.) New York. 1874.

BANKER'S Common Place Book. (192 pp. 12mo.)
New York. 1869.

BANKER'S ALMANAC for 1873. (8 vo.) New York. 1873.
Illustrated with cuts from Homans' "Coin Book."

BARBER, J. W. Connecticut Historical Collections. (8vo.)
New Haven. 1849.

——— Historical Collections. History and Antiquities of every town in Massachusetts. (8vo.) Worcester. 1841.

BARRA, E. J. "Something about Coins." (31 pp. 16mo.)
San Francisco. 1863.

BISSELL & Co., Geo. P. Coin Book issued by the Banking House of, Hartford. 1873.
Contains a number of illustrations from Homans' "Coin Book."

BOARD of EDUCATION. 14th Annual Report of the—City and County of New York. (8vo.) New York. 1856.

BOYD, Andrew. " Lincoln Bibliography." (175 pp. sm. 4to.)
Albany. 1870.

BROADHEAD, J. R. History of the State of New York.
(801 pp. 8vo.) New York. 1853.

—— The same, 2d Volume. New York. 1871.

BUSHNELL, C. I. An Arrangement of Tradesmen's Cards, Political Tokens, Medals, etc.. of the United States.
(124 pp. 8vo.) New York. 1858.

—— An Historical account of the first three business Tokens issued in the City of New York. (18 pp. 8vo.)
New York. 1859.

CAMPBELL, Charles. History of the Colony and Ancient Dominion of Virginia. (765 pp. Royal 8vo.)
Philadelphia. 1860.

CATALOGUE of the Massachusetts State Library. (8vo.)
Boston. 1858.

CHALMERS, George. Introduction to the History of the Revolt of the American Colonies. (2 vols. in one.) Boston. 1845.

CHAMBERS Encyclopedia. (10 vols. 8vo.) Philadelphia. 1870.

CHAMPION, Frank. Campaign Hand Book and Citizens' Manual. (Illustrated 8vo.) Hartford. 1872.

CHARTER and By-Laws of the ATHENÆUM of Philadelphia. (8vo.)
Philadelphia. 1820.

Cincinnati Industrial Exposition, 1873. Report of the Board of Commissioners. (269 pp. 8vo.) Cincinnati. 1873.

CIRCULAR LETTER. In Relation to American Medals and Cabinet Coins. Mint of the United States, Phia. (12 pp. 12mo.)
Philadelphia. 1861.

CLARK, F. W. Weights, Measures, and Money of all Nations.
(117 pp. 8vo.) New York. 1876.

This work, though dated 1876 was issued in 1875.

COIN and STAMP JOURNAL. Published by A. B. Mason.
Chicago. 1866.

Twelve numbers of this little 5¼x8¼ bantling of 4 pp. each sufficed to kill it.

COIN AND STAMP JOURNAL. Kansas City. Mo. (4to.)
1875 and 1876.

W. E. WINNER was the publisher of this lively little monthly. Its first number is dated January, 1875. In July, 1876, it passed into the hands of Mr. J. J. CASEY of New York, by whom it is now published.

COLDEN, Cadwallader C. Memoir prepared at the request of a committee of the Common Council of the City of New York at the completion of the New York Canals. (410 pp. 4to.)
New York. 1825.

On pp. 346 and 347 is a description of and particulars relating to the Erie Canal Medals.

COLUMBIAN MAGAZINE. (See April number, page 200.) 1788.

COMPLETE GUIDE to the great EXPOSITION, Louisville, Ky.
(46 pp. 8vo.) Louisville. 1872.

CONYBEARE, W. J. and HOWSON, J. S. Life and Epistles of St. Paul. (2 vols. 8vo., Illustrated.) New York. 1858.

COOK, Henry. "Coin and Medal Circular." (12 pp. 12mo.)
Boston. 1864.

The copy in my possession is interleaved, whether all were thus issued or not, I am uncertain.

———— Hand Book of Coins and Medals, (16 pp. 16mo.)
Boston. 1874.

CROSBY, S. S. "The EARLY COINS OF AMERICA," and the laws governing their issue, comprising also descriptions of the Washington pieces, the Anglo-American tokens, many pieces of unknown origin of the 17th and 18th centuries, and the first Patterns of the U. S. Mint. Published by the Author. (384 pp. Illustrated.) Boston. 1875.

This recent publication is a valuable acquisition to numismatic science in this country, whether as a work of reference or for the study of the subject matter, it will be found to be the fullest and most reliable work on "Colonials" yet published.
Mr. Sylvester S. Crosby, its able author, was born in Charlestown, N. H., September 2d, 1837. He has for many years been a resident of Boston, Mass., where he is the senior partner of one of its leading jewelry establishments. Mr. Crosby commenced collecting in 1857, and his cabinet now contains many of the finest

and rarest of the Colonial pieces, which series he has made one of his specialties, as he has also of the "Washington pieces," of which he also has quite a number of the scarcest. Of the regular issues of the U.S. Mint in copper, he has secured many of the great number of varieties. Mint Medals and Pattern pieces, as well as of the miscellaneous issues from other dies, he has not left unnoticed, his cabinet containing quite a select variety. To sum up in a few words, American pieces from whatever source, are to him objects of his desire, solicitude, and care.

"Curiosity Shop." Published monthly by W. S. Haines (or Haines & Olcutt.) Chicago.

This little publication commenced in July and ceased in Dec. 1865.

DA COSTA, B. F. Rambles in Mount Desert. (8vo.) New York. 1871.

Deakins' Old Curiosity Shop. Chicago, Ill. 1871.

Messrs. W. H. Deakin issued a single number of 4 Pages, with the above title, in August, 1871.

DE PEYSTER, J. WATTS. Eulogy of Lennart Torstenson. (36 pp. 4to.) New York. 1872.

Has an account and description of various medals.

DE PEYSTER, J. WATTS. History of the Life of Leonard Torstenson. Poughkeepsie. 1855.

DE PEYSTER, J. WATTS. Medals and Coins of Carausius. (335 pp. 8vo.) Poughkeepsie. 1858.

DESCRIPTION of the Medals presented by OSCAR, King of Sweden and Norway, to Gen. J. WATTS DE PEYSTER. Privately printed. (6 pp.) New York. April 17, 1857.

✓ DICKESON, MONTROVILLE W. The American Numismatic Manual. (4to.) Philadelphia. 1859.

A second edition was issued.

DICKESON, MONTROVILLE W. THE AMERICAN NUMISMATIC MANUAL of the currency or money of the aborigines and Colonial State and United States Coins, with Historical and descriptive notices of each coin or series. 3d Edition. (271 pp. 4to.) Published by J. B. Lippincott & Co. Phia. 1865.

This is one of the most valuable books published on American coins and is well illustrated.

This edition has a supplement added to the text of the previous editions.

DILLAWAY, CHARLES K. Roman Antiquities and Mythology.

DISOSWAY, G. P. National Magazine. (192 pp. 8vo.)
New York. 1854.

DOWLING, JOHN. The History of Romanism from the earliest
corruptions of Christianity to the present time.
(672 pp. 8vo.) New York. 1845.

DUBOIS, WILLIAM E. Pledges of History. A brief account of
the Collection of Coins belonging to the Mint of the U. S.,
more particularly of the Antique specimens. Illustrated.
(138 pp. 12mo.) Philadelphia. 1846.
An edition of but 150 copies was privately printed.

✓ ECKFELDT AND DUBOIS. · A Manual of Gold and Silver Coins
of all Nations, struck within the past century. Published
at the Assay Office of the U. S. Mint. Illustrated by Joseph Saxton. (220 pp. 4to.) Philadelphia. 1842.

ECKFELDT AND DUBOIS. A Manual of Gold and Silver Coins of
all Nations, struck within the past century. With a Supplement. (4to.) Philadelphia. 1849.
A republication of the work of 1842 with the omission of the Plates and the addition of the Supplement.

ECKFELDT AND DUBOIS. New Varieties of Gold and Silver
Coins, Counterfeit Coins and Bullion with mint values.
(61 pp. 12mo.) Philadelphia. 1850.

✓ FELT, JOSEPH B. An Historical Account of Massachusetts
Currency. Illustrated. (259 pp. 8vo.) Boston. 1839.

FLEET'S Pocket Almanac. (12mo.) Boston. 1789.

FORCE, PETER. American Archives, 5th Series.
(See Vol. I.) Folio. Washington. 1851.

FOWLE, D. "An exact table to bring old tenor into lawful
money. Also a table to know the value of Pistoles, Guin-
eas, Johannes and double Johannes, Moydores, English
Crowns, Shillings and copper halfpence at the rate of Dollars
at six shillings a piece, at which invariable value they are
fixed by a late act of this government. The act to be in
force from and after the 31st of March, 1750." Third edition.
(12 pp., size 3x1½ inches.) Boston. 1750.

FRANCIS, JOHN W. Old New York. (400 pp. 8vo.)
New York. 1866.

FRENCH, JAMES. Massachusetts State Record. (280 pp. 8vo.)
Boston. 1847.

FROST, JOHN. American Naval Biography. (440 pp. 8vo.)
Philadelphia. 1844.

GALLATIN, ALBERT. " Letter from the Secretary of the Treasury transmitting a report prepared in obedience to the act entitled "An act regulating the currency of Foreign Coins in the United States." (8 pp. 8vo.) Washington. 1809.

GREEN, G. W. The Works of Joseph Addison. (5 vols. 8vo.)
New York. 1853.

GREENHOW, R. History of Oregon and California. (8vo.)
Boston. 1844·

GROUX, DANIEL E. Prospectus of an important work in three volumes to be called Numismatical History of the United States, &c., &c. (16 pp. 8vo.) Boston. 1856.

> The work never was issued.

GROUX, DANIEL E. Opinions of the Press concerning a beautiful collection of Medals and Coins also Books on Coins, exhibited during the Month of May, 1856, at the rooms of the Mercantile Library Association. Boston. 1856.

> A slip about 6 inches wide and 24 inches long containing extracts from the Boston Papers.

GROUX, DANIEL E. Final Arrangements for the Sale of Shares. For the Medals and Coins. Boston. May 29, 1856.

> A small Sheet Circular, soliciting subscriptions to his Lottery scheme for disposing of his collection.

HAZARD, SAMUEL. Communication of, to the Board of Trustees of the Second Presbyterian Church. (16 pp. 8vo.)
Philadelphia. 1864.

HARPER'S MAGAZINE.   New York. 1860.
    See numbers for February and March.

HARRIS, L. Handbook of Coins and Medals, containing a few
    remarks on the American Series of Coins and Medals, with
    a little brief advice to the inexperienced collector.
    (23 pp. 12mo.)   New York. 1875.
    Mr. Harris also issued a circular headed "Old Coins! Old Coins!" L. Harris
    of New York, will be here for one day, and will pay a HIGH PRICE for all kinds
    of old coins of rare dates." Evidently a peddler's circular, as he also offers to
    "Sell old Coins."

HEBREW CUSTOMS. (88 pp. 8vo.)   Philadelphia. n. d.

HICKOX, J. H.   A Historical Account of American Coinage.
    (151 pp. 8vo.)   '   Albany. 1858.

HISTORICAL MAGAZINE.   New York. 1857.
    This magazine, which was commenced in 1857 and is still being published, con-
    tains many articles and descriptions of Coins and Medals interesting to numis-
    matists.

HISTORICAL SOCIETY of New York Proceedings.   (8vo.)
                                           New York. 1848.
    On p. 153 is an acknowledgement of donations of Coins.

HISTORICAL SOCIETY of New York. Collections. New York.
    (See Vol. III,   p. 387.)

HODGE'S Coin Chart Manual. Issued by Hodge's Journal of
    Finance and Bank Reporter.   (50 pp. 8vo.)
                                           New York. 1856.
    Illustrated with many wood-cuts of coins.

HOLMES. Abiel, Annals of America. (2 vols. 8vo.)
                                           Cambridge. 1829.

HOMES, HENRY A.   Observations on the Design and Import of
    Medals. (8 pp. 8vo.)   Albany. 1863.

HOUGH, F. B. Washingtoniana, or Memorials of the Death
    of George Washington. Illustrated.
    Printed for W. E. Woodward. (272 pp. 8vo.)   .
                                           Roxbury. 1865.
    Contains, pages 278 to 291, a description by W. E. Woodward of some Wash-
    ington Medals.
    The edition was 200 copies 8vo. and 91 copies 4to., 6 of the latter printed on
    drawing paper.

HOUGH, F. B.   History of Lewis County.

JACOBS, WILLIAM.   Historical Enquiries in precious metals.
(427 pp. 8vo.)   Philadelphia.   1832.

JOHNSON.   History and Reminiscences.
On page 4 is an account of the "Carolina Medal."

JONES, GEORGE F.   The Coin Collector's Manual, containing a
description of the Gold, Silver, Copper and other coins of
the U. S., etc.   (41 pp. Quarto.)   Philadelphia.   1860.

KURIOSITI KABINET.   A little monthly periodical, issued by Mr.
WILLIAM P. BROWN.
He published the first number in September, 1870, discontinued it in 1873, and
has now (1876) re-commenced its issue, *semi-occasionally*. The first page of each
of the former periodicals was published in phonetic type, on two sizes of paper.

LEWIS, WINSLOW.   Address to the Boston Numismatic Society.
(13 pp. small 4to.)   Boston.   1866.

LINDEMAN, HENRY R.   Circular letter in relation to American
Medals and Cabinet Coins.   (12 pp. 12mo.)
                                                  Philadelphia.   1867.

"LIST of NAMES contained in the Subscription Book up to
June 1, 1856, in chronological order."   Boston.   1856.
Contains a list of the names of "persons who have testified to the merits and
value of the collections of Medals and Coins" (Daniel E. Groux's) and "Names of
Shareholders in Boston and Vicinity."
A sheet slip, about 4x12 inches.

LONG ISLAND HISTORICAL SOCIETY.   1st Annual Report.
(48 pp. 8vo.)   Brooklyn.   1863.

LONG ISLAND HISTORICAL SOCIETY.   3d Annual Report.
(70 pp. 8vo.)   Brooklyn.   1866.

LOSSING, BENSON J.   The American Historical Record and
Repertory of Notes and Queries.   Concerning the history
and antiquities of America, and Biography of Americans.
Published monthly. Commenced in 1872. Continued during 1873-4.
                                                  Philadelphia.   1872.

LOSSING, B. J.   Pictorial Field Book of the Revolution.
(2 vols. Royal 8vo.)   New York.   1851.

Lossing, B. J.   Pictorial Field Book of the War of 1812.
(Royal 8vo.)   New York.   1868.

Lossing, B. J.   Pictorial History of the Civil War.
(Royal 8vo.)   Philadelphia.   1866.

ʸ Maris, Edward.   Varieties of the Copper Issues of the U. S.
Mint in the year 1794 by Edward Maris, M. D.
(15 pp. 8vo.)   Philadelphia.   1869.
    An excellent little work, worthy the emulation of numismatists.   A second
    edition was issued in 1870.

Mason's Coin and Stamp Collector's Magazine.   (8vo.)
                                      Philadelphia.   1867 to 1873.
    This Magazine, which commenced in April 1867, was continued until 1873, when
    it ceased publication with its 7th volume.   It was one of the best of the many at-
    tempts made by an individual to establish a monthly of a numismatic character.

Massachusetts Historical Society.   Collections.   Third Series.   (300 pp. 8vo.)   Boston.   1837.
    In Vol. VI. on p. 286 et seq. are descriptions of American medals by J. Francis
    Fisher, Esq.

Memoirs of the American Academy of Arts and Sciences.
    See Vol. III.   Part I., pp. 195--196.)

Mercantile Library Association, St. Louis.   Thirteenth Annual Report.   (41 pp. 8vo.)   St. Louis.   1859.
    On p. 23 is an acknowledgement of donations, and of a prospective large do-
    nation.

Merchants' and Bankers' Almanac.   (234 pp. 8vo.)
                                      New York.   1869.

Metallic Money, its Value and its Functions.   (14 pp. 8vo.)
                                      Philadelphia.   1841.

Metropolitan Coin Book.   Published by Gwynne & Day.
Illustrated.   (46 pp. 4to.)   New York.   1860.

ʸ Miller, Matthew T.   The Coins of the World.   Illustrated.
Published by Matthew T. Miller.   (74 pp. Post 8vo.)
                                      Philadelphia.   1849.

Mickley, J. J.   Dates of United States Coins and their Rarity.
(4 pp. 4to.)   Philadelphia.   1858.

MILLS, ROBERT. Guide to the Capitol at Washington, and to the National Executive Offices of the U. S. (86 pp. 8vo.)

Washington. 1854.

Vide pp. 26 and 27.

MORGAN, CHARLES. Monies, Currency and Banking.

New York. 1875.

MORRIS, ROBERT. Medallic History of Commodus, Emperor of Rome, A. D., 180 to 192. (48 pp. 8vo.) New York. 1873.

MORRIS, ROBERT. Light in Masonry. A Monthly Magazine.

New York. 1873.

(But 4 numbers were issued.)

MORRIS, ROBERT. Freemasonry in the Holy Land. (608 pp. Royal 8vo.) New York. 1872.

MORRIS, ROBERT. Our Monthly.

A magazine commenced in 1870. But few numbers were published.

NEW YORK. Journal of the Assembly. (8vo.) 1787.

See page 78.

NEW YORK STATE LIBRARY. Annual Report of the Trustees of the. (222 pp. 8vo.) Albany. 1854.

Vide pp. 165 and 222.

NORTON, CHARLES B. Literary Letter No. 1. (41 pp. 4to.) Illustrated. New York. 1857.

NORTON, CHARLES B. Literary Letter No. 2. Comprising American papers of Interest, and a catalogue of the largest collection of rare and valuable autographs, coins, medals, maps, etc. (46 pp. 4to.) New York. 1858.

NORTON, CHARLES B. Literary Letter No. 3. (66 pp. 4to.)

New York. 1859.

NORTON, CHARLES B. Literary Letter No. 4. (52 pp. 4to.)

New York. 1859.

NORTON, CHARLES B. Literary Letter No. 1. New Series.

New York. 1860.

NUMISMATIC SOCIETY of Philadelphia. *American Store Cards.*
(423 lots. 16 pp. Quarto.) Philadelphia. 1858.

Messrs. M. W. Collet, J. L. Hodge and A. B. Taylor were appointed a committee to prepare a list of Store Cards issued in this country. Though useful at that time. the above-named Society would probably find more honor than profit in issuing a revised copy. The above has, like an old city directory, become useless.

NUMISMATIC SOCIETY of Philadelphia. Constitution and By-Laws of the. (11 pp. 12mo.) Philadelphia. 1858.

OGDEN, R W. "An Enquiry into the Early History of Money." New Orleans. 1870.

An address read before the "New Orleans Academy of Sciences," April 11th, 1870. 100 copies were afterwards privately printed.

OGDEN, R. W. "An Enquiry into the Early Monetary History of the American Colonies." 7pp. 8vo. New Orleans. 1870.

An address read Oct. 31, 1870, before the "New Orleans Academy of Sciences." 100 copies were afterwards printed for private distribution.

Mr. Ogden, the able author of the above two numismatic pamphlets is an old, well-known numismatist of New Orleans, whose collection of coins was at one time much more extensive than at present. The death of an elder son whose tastes were much similar to those of his respected father and the events of late years having led Mr. Ogden to part with a portion of his collection, but not his tastes for numismatics; which, with his ability, has been recognized and honored by the "New Orleans Academy of Sciences," in the placing of Mr. Ogden as chairman of the "Scientific Section, Numismatics, Antiquarian researches, and Ethnology." He is a corresponding member of the American Numismatic and Archæological Society of New York, as also of other learned societies.

PEABODY ACADEMY of SCIENCE. 1st Annual Report.
(103 pp. 8vo.) Salem. 1869.

PEABODY ACADEMY of SCIENCE. Second and Third Annual Reports for the years 1869 & 1870. (109 pp. 8vo.)
Salem. 1871.

PETERSON BROS., T. B. Coins of the World. Philadelphia.

PETTIGREW, T. J. Superstitions connected with the History and Practice of Medicine and Surgery. (213 pp. 8vo.)
Philadelphia.

This book has a plate of the obv. and rev. of four "ROYAL TOUCH PIECES," and a description of them on p. 162 *et seq.*

PHELPS, NOAH A. History of Simsbury, Granby and Canton.
Hartford. 1845.

PHELPS, RICHARD H.   History of Newgate of Connecticut.
(151 pp. 8vo.)   Albany.   1860.

PHILLIPS Jr., HENRY.   Pleasures of Numismatic Science.
(14 pp. 8vo.)   Philadelphia.   1867.

PRIME, W. C.   Medals and Seals, Ancient and Modern.
(292 pp. 4to.   Illustrated.)   New York.   1861.
  A useful and instructive work to novices in numismatic science.

PROCEEDINGS of the Numismatic and Antiquarian Society of
  Philadelphia, from May, 1865, to December 31, 1866.
(160 pp. 8vo.)   Philadelphia.   1867.
  25 Copies printed on large paper and 250 in 8vo.

RANDOLPH, T. J.   Life, Memoirs and Correspondence of Thomas Jefferson.   (4 vols. 8vo.)   Charlottesville.   1829.

RECEPTION of VOLUNTEERS.   Published by authority of the
  Board of Aldermen.   (145 pp. 8vo.)   New York.   1850.

REPORT and COLLECTIONS of the State Historical Society of
  Wisconsin for the years 1857 and 1858.
(Vol. IV. 508 pp. 8vo.)   Madison.   1859.
  See pp. 28 and 59.

REPORT of the COMMITTEE appointed on the 27th of November
  last, to enquire into the expediency of amending the laws
  which regulate the Coins of the United States, and foreign
  coins, etc.   (10 pp. 8vo.)   Washington.   1819.

REPORT of the Joint Special Committee of the Common Council, appointed for the purpose of making suitable arrangements for the reception of Major-General Scott on his return from Mexico, and to tender to him the hospitalities of
  the city.   (66 pp. 8vo.)   New York.   1849.
  Contains a description of the Medal presented to General Scott by the city.

REPORT of the Trustees of the New York State Library.
(80 pp. 8vo.)   Albany.   1858.
  Coins on pp. 21 and 77.

RHEES, WM. J.   An account of the Smithsonian Institution, its
  Founder, Building, Operations, etc.   (74 pp. 8vo.)
                                             Washington.   1859.

RHODE ISLAND NUMISMATIC ASSOCIATION. Constitution and By-Laws. Providence. 1866.

RHODE ISLAND NUMISMATIC ASSOCIATION. Constitution and By-Laws. Revised Edition. (10 pp. 16mo.)
Providence. 1868.

RIDDEL, J. L. A Monograph of the Silver Dollar. Good and Bad. Illustrated with 425 varieties of Dollars and 87 varieties of Half Dollars, etc. (371 pp. 8vo.)
New Orleans. 1845.

ROWELL, C. S. W. Alloying Table. Value of Gold and Silver coins, etc. A broadside sheet. New York. 1838.

RUNKEL, WILLIAM M. United States Mint. Philadelphia. 1870.

SATTERLEE, ALFRED H. An arrangement of Medals and Tokens struck in honor of the Presidents of the United States, and of the Presidential Candidates. (84 pp. 8vo.)
New York. 1862.

A similar work which will correct the errors which have been found to exist in the above, and include issues to date will be both useful and instructive.

SIMMS, J. R. History of Schoharie Co., N. Y. 8vo.
Albany. 1845.

See pp. 596–598.

SHERMAN, MORGAN and RUGGLES. Reports of, on a Bill to establish a Uniform Coinage. Washington. 1868.

SLADE, WM. Vermont State Papers. 8vo.
Middlebury. 1823.

See p. 509.

SLAFTON, Rev. EDWARD F. The Vermont Coinage, reprinted from the first volume of the collections of the Vermont Historical Society. Two Plates. (30 pp. 8vo.)
Montpelier. 1870.

50 copies printed.

SMITH, H. I. The Merchants' and Bankers' Almanac for 1872. (8vo.) New York. 1872.

SMITH, J. J. and WATSON, J. F. American Historical and Literary Curiosities, with a variety of Reliques, Antiquities, &c. Illustrated. 4to. Philadelphia. 1861.

SNOWDEN, J. R. A Description of Ancient and Modern Coins in the Cabinet Collection at the Mint of the United States. Illustrated. (412 pp. 8vo.) Philadelphia. 1860.

SNOWDEN, J. R. Coins of the Bible. Enlarged Edition. (94 pp. 12 mo.) Philadelphia. 1864.

SNOWDEN, J. R. International Coinage. (10 pp.) Philadelphia. 1870.
A reprint of an article in Lippincott's Magazine for January.

✓ SNOWDEN, JAMES R. The Medallic Memorials of Washington in the Mint of the United States. (Illustrated. 203 pp. 4to.) Philadelphia. 1861.

STICKNEY, M. A. Notes on American Coinage.

STOUT, JAMES V. A table of the intrinsic value of the current money of every nation. No date. New York.
An engraved broadside sheet. Probably printed 1820 to 1830.

✓ STROBRIDGE, WILLIAM H. "A descriptive Catalogue of the Seavey Collection of American Coins, the property of Loring G. Parmelee of Boston." University Press, Cambridge. (63 pp. illustrated. 8vo.) Cambridge. 1873.
150 copies were printed on tinted paper and the price fixed at $3.00 each. Those desiring copies may address the owner of the collection, who has probably "a few more left of the same sort."

TAYLOR'S Gold and Silver Coin Examiner. New York. 1837.

THATCHER. American Medical Biography. Boston. 1828.
(See Vol I. p. 229.)

"THE AMERICAN COIN and STAMP REVIEW." A monthly, published by "The Keystone Stamp Association," commenced May and ceased in August, 1871, with an issue of 4 numbers, 16 pages, at Allentown, Pennsylvania.

THE BANKER'S COMMON PLACE BOOK. (192 pp. 12mo.) New York. 1869.

THE BANKER'S MAGAZINE for 1870, 1871. New York. 1871.
"THE COIN CIRCULAR." Published by George A. Dillingham.

Issued its first number in March, 1875, and is still publishing. *Success to you!*

"THE COLLECTOR," Newburgh, N. Y. Published by David W. Jagger.

A monthly of 4 pages, commenced Nov. 1871, and ceased with April 1872, having issued 6 numbers.

"THE COIN COLLECTOR'S JOURNAL."

This new aspirant for numismatic favor commenced its existence in December 1875. Edited by Mr. EDWARD FROSSARD and published by that enterprising firm, Messrs. J. W. SCOTT & Co., of New York, at $1.00 per annum.

"THE COLLECTOR'S GUIDE."

Was another of those little 5¼x8¼ ephemeral publications, which was issued partly at Newport, R. I., and partly at Cambridge, Mass., by Messrs. Gould & Canfield, during 1866, commencing in May, at the former place, and in October at the latter place. 8 numbers in all, of 36 Pages.

"THE COIN AND STAMP JOURNAL."

Published by the National Stamp Co., Meriden, Conn., commenced Jan. 1868, and died a natural death after three months' illness, from a total dose of 16 pages 5¼x8¼ inches.

THE COLLECTOR'S REVIEW. A little monthly published by Edward M. Reed & Co. Toledo, O. January, 1873.

I know not whether more than one number was issued.

THE CURIOSITY HUNTER.

A monthly published *semi-occasionally*, commencing September, 1872, and died, I believe, after issuing No. 7 of Vol. 2.

" THE DECORAH NUMISMATIC JOURNAL. Published Quarterly by Cooley & Holway." Decorah, Iowa. 1875.

In its No. 4 it announces that "This Journal will not be published another year." It is to be regretted that it did not succeed.

"THE OLD CURIOSITY SHOP." A monthly Magazine. Published by Harlow E. Woodward. Boston. 1871 and 1872.

Vol. I., No. 3, contains an article on the antiquity of money by W. H. STROBRIDGE.

THE SPECTATOR

Contains an article on Oriental Numismatics. 5 Nos. only were published. See Jencks & Paine's Catalogue, December 10th, 1866.

"THE STAMP AND COIN TRADER."

A Monthly, was published by the Globe Stamp Co. at Rockford, Illinois, who issued six numbers, commencing in December 1873, and ceased therewith its June 1874 number. It is, I believe, still issuing from Janesville, Wisconsin.

THOMPSON'S COIN CHART MANUAL. New York. 1836.

This well-known illustrated annual which has been published for so many years, has now fallen into the hands of Messrs. J. W. Scott & Co., the well-known Coin and Stamp Dealers in New York City, who will issue it in an entire new dress. It illustrates many hundred coins.

UNICHE—The Mysteries of Isis, or the Science of Mythematics. Issued by John A. Bell, Sassafras Fork, Granville Co., N. C. 8vo. New York. 1858.

VALENTINE, D. T. Manual of the Corporation of the City of New York for 1859. New York. 1859.

Has an illustrated article by C. I. Bushnell, Esq.

VERMONT HISTORICAL MAGAZINE.

Vol. VI., p. 228., has an article by Sheldon on the History of the town of Rupert, where the Vermont tokens were struck.

VERMONT HISTORICAL SOCIETY'S Collections. Vol. I. 8vo.

WALDEN, P. E. Compilation of the Tariff Act of the Confederate States of America. Approved May 1st, 1861. (282 pp. 8vo.) New Orleans. 1861.

WALLER, PERCIVAL. The Universal Library of Literature and Illustrated Mirror of the World. (488 pp. 4to.) Philadelphia. 1860.

WEIGHTS, MEASURES and COINS. "Extracts from the report of the international committee, on." (47 pp. 8vo.) Washington. 1870.

WHITE, S. S Dental Catalogue. Philadelphia. 1862.

✓ WHARTON, JOSEPH. Project for reorganizing the small coinage of the United States. (24 pp. 8vo.) Philadelphia. 1864.

WILLIAMSON, JOSEPH. Castine and the old coins found there (22 pp. 8vo.) Portland. 1859.

WISCONSIN STATE HISTORICAL SOCIETY. First Annual Report of, for the year 1854. Vol. I. (160 pp. 8vo.)
Madison. 1855.

Vide page 11.

WOODWORTH, JOHN. Reminiscences of Troy from its Settlement in 1790 to 1807, with remarks on its Commerce, Enterprise, Improvements, State of Political parties and sketches of Individual Character, written at the request of several gentlemen of Troy. 2d Edition, with notes, explanatory, Biographical, Historical and Antiquarian. (112 pp. 4to.)
Albany. 1860.

On p. 80 is a notice of the issue of "Church Pennies."

WOODWARD, W. E. A List of Washington Memorial Medals. Privately printed. (16 pp. 8vo.)   Roxbury. 1865.

Of this work but 50 copies were printed, 12 of which were on drawing paper.

WYATT, THOMAS. History of the Kings of France, containing the principal incidents in their lives from the foundation of the monarchy to Louis Phillippe. 72 Portraits. (252 pp. 8vo.)   Philadelphia. 1846.

WYATT, THOMAS. Memoirs of the Generals, Commodores, and other Commanders who distinguished themselves during the Wars of the Revolution and 1812. (Pub. by Carey & Hart.) Illustrated by 82 fine Steel Engravings. (315 pp. 8vo)
Philadelphia. 1848.

ZABRISKIE, ANDREW C. A Descriptive catalogue of the Political and Memorial Medals struck in honor of Abraham Lincoln, sixteenth President of the United States. Only seventy-five copies printed. Printed for the Author. (32 pp. 8vo. on fine tinted paper.)   New York. 1873.

Mr. Zabriskie omitted to catalogue several medals which had been struck, some of them in terra cotta, wood, green clay, and SOAP, as well as a number of others which did not exist when he wrote his catalogue; with these (important!) exceptions his catalogue will be found a useful one to a person making a collection of the Lincoln series of medals.

Eric:

Note Bottom Half

of Page 86

www.ingramcontent.com/pod-product-compliance
Lightning Source LLC
Chambersburg PA
CBHW030613270326
41927CB00007B/1161